Government Requirements
of Small Business

The Battelle Human Affairs Research Centers Series

The White-Collar Challenge to Nuclear Safeguards
edited by Herbert Edelhertz and *Marilyn Walsh*

Government Requirements of Small Business
edited by Roland J. Cole and *Philip D. Tegeler*

A National Strategy for White-Collar Crime Enforcement
edited by Herbert Edelhertz and *Charles Rogovin*

Government Requirements of Small Business

Roland J. Cole
Philip D. Tegeler
Battelle Human Affairs Research Centers

LexingtonBooks
D.C. Heath and Company
Lexington, Massachusetts
Toronto

Library of Congress Cataloging in Publication Data

Cole, Roland J
Government requirements of small business.

Bibliography: p.
1. Small business—United States. 2. Small business—Law and legisla-tion—Economic aspects—United States. I. Tegeler, Philip D., joint author.
II. Title.
HD2346.U5C55   338.6'42'0973   79-3046
ISBN 0-669-03307-3

International Standard Book Number: 0-669-03307-3

Library of Congress Catalog Card Number: 79-3046

To the owners and managers of small businesses throughout the United States.

Contents

List of Figures

List of Tables

Acknowledgments

The research for this report was done in close collaboration with Private Sector Initiatives of Seattle, Washington, as is discussed in detail in the report. Financial support for the research came from the Medina Foundation of Seattle, Washington.

Selected individuals from these and other groups became advisors who were consulted at a number of points in the course of this research. The advisors included Bill Leckenby, Joe Garcia, John Behnke, Ralph Munro, Fred Shanaman, and Len Saari of PSI; Greg Barlow of the Medina Foundation; Bill Robinson of AWB; Gary Smith of the Independent Business Association; Robert Caldwell of the regional office of the Small Business Administration; Glenn Pascal of the Washington State Research Council; Bill Larson of the Puget Sound Council of Governments; William Alberts and Karl Vesper of the Graduate School of Business Administration at the University of Washington; Bill Wilkerson of Eisenhower, Carlson, Newlands, Reba, Henrist, and Quinn; Dave Klick of Northwest Food Processors Association; Carol Aaron of Seattle Chamber of Commerce; Bill Lotto of the Economic Development Council of Puget Sound; Saul Arrington of the Washington State Department of Licensing; Doug Clark of the Washington State Department of Commerce and Economic Development, and Cathy Shreve of the Seattle Department of Community Development.

In addition to those individuals and groups, we would like to acknowledge a special debt to six other people here at Battelle: first, two supervisors—John Rasmussen and Dick Schuller—who were willing to roll up their sleeves and join us in the trenches as colleagues; second, two editors—Shelley Smolkin and Vivian Hedrich—who leavened their insistence on consistency with sympathy for the distractions we authors were facing; and third, two typists—Sandy Smith and Susan Morrison—who responded to innumerable corrections and tight deadlines with effectiveness and good spirits.

1 Introduction

The Problem of Government Requirements

Federal, state, and local governments attempt to achieve many social goals by regulating private businesses through statutes and regulations. These attempts have increased substantially in recent years. At the federal level they include requirements administered by the Equal Employment Opportunity Commission, the Environmental Protection Agency, the Consumer Product Safety Commission, and the Occupational Safety and Health Administration. State and local governments have imposed requirements in the same areas at an increasing rate.[1] As a consequence, government requirements are a matter of increasing concern to business.

One major problem of business is that these requirements, even though socially valuable, impose costs on business operation. Some of the costs are related to changes in business practices necessitated by the requirements. These might include installation of pollution controls, compliance with safety requirements, and training or retraining of employees. Other costs are related to required changes in the procedures used by business in its interactions with government. Related tasks might include filing reports to demonstrate compliance with regulations and keeping special records for government reporting purposes. A third set of costs is related to the interpretation of governmental requirements. Included are the costs of learning which requirements apply and what they mean and the legal and administrative costs of settling disagreements with the regulators.

Some of these costs are probably unavoidable; however, others can and should be avoided. Some of the avoidable costs stem from requirements that may create one problem while trying to solve another, such as restrictions on travel time for trucks that increase congestion and noise rather than decreasing it. Other avoidable costs stem not from the requirements themselves, but from the way they are administered. Many of these avoidable costs fall into the interpretation category just described: they stem from insufficient publicity or explanation of requirements and procedures or from poorly functioning procedures for resolving disputes. A recurrent example is the debate over the meaning of "best available technology" for pollution control.

Businessmen and others often assume that government requirements impose a disproportionate burden on small businesses—meaning businesses independently owned (usually closely held), nondominant in their markets, and with

1

few employees (less than 50) or relatively low annual revenue (less than $1 million). Small businesses are less likely to have the resources to monitor, interpret, and respond to changing government requirements. They are also apt to be harder hit when a serious dispute arises. A lawsuit that would slow down a large firm may destroy a small one. Costs for new equipment, costs of additional administrative labor or expertise, and the more elusive costs of wasted time or diverted resources all combine to create a disproportionate drain on managerial time and increase managerial frustrations for the small businessman.

This book is an attempt to document the nature and magnitude of the costs imposed by government requirements on small business. It also identifies some mechanisms that might be useful to reduce these costs.

The Project on Small Business

Project Design

Although issues related to the impacts of government requirements on small business have received public attention (see the hearings listed in the bibliography), few previous attempts have been made to identify and quantify the impacts. One reason for this information gap is the limited resources available to the small business community for research. Yet the research could have tremendous value—by one definition of a small business (less than fifty employees), 95 percent of the businesses in Washington state are small, and these businesses employ one-third of the state's workforce.

Part of the problem of documenting impacts has been the reluctance of small businesses to participate in research activities that seemed remote from their day-to-day needs. To confront the problems faced by small businesses because of government requirements, Battelle Human Affairs Research Centers (HARC) and Private Sector Initiatives (PSI) formed a working relationship and launched a three-phase, action-oriented research project. Both parties hoped that a partnership between a social science research institute and an association of business and professional leaders would be more effective in this area than either one would be working alone. The Medina Foundation provided support for the research.

Objectives

The ultimate goals of this research program are to reduce the costs imposed on small business, to keep the unavoidable costs at a minimum, and to do away with as many as possible of the avoidable costs. However, we cannot hope to reach these long-range goals immediately. Therefore, the project is designed to achieve a series of sequential objectives that should lead to the final outcome. The tasks to achieve these objectives are divided into three phases.

The goal of phase I is to identify and analyze the costs of government requirements in enough detail to guide reform efforts. This book is the result of that phase. The goal of phase II is to design a series of measures for both the public and private sectors to reduce the avoidable costs. The design activity will directly apply the knowledge gained from phase I. The goal of phase III is to ensure that the suggested reforms are at least given a serious hearing in the public and private sectors and to do whatever is possible to see that they are adopted. The third phase will also include monitoring the effectiveness of the adopted recommendations.

The project began in the fall of 1977 and is expected to continue through 1979 or 1980, at the rate of roughly one phase per year. All those involved expect that the information in this book can be used by both private and public organizations to work toward reducing the unproductive or otherwise undesirable side effects of government requirements on small business.

Contents of this Book

Chapter 1 has described the problem and the research project. Chapter 2 presents background for the research, including a very brief history of the problem, a brief review of previous research, and a discussion of the approach and initial hypotheses. Chapter 3 outlines the specific objectives of the research. Chapter 4 discusses the methodology in detail. We devoted special attention to being systematic in this area, because most of the related research is not very systematic. Chapters 5-7 present results of the research in terms of answers to the questions posed by the specific objectives. Chapter 8 sets forth two kinds of policy implications: general guidelines for all attempts to reduce the costs of government requirements and a list of suggestions that meet those guidelines. The appendixes contain questionnaires used in the mail surveys, as well as data that were particularly valuable for their own sake and are not readily available elsewhere, such as the reports from our case studies of small businesses. Other appendixes contain analyses that are important, but too detailed for the text.

Project Boundaries

In order to achieve these objectives within the limits of our resources, we set several explicit boundaries on the research. First, and most important, this study examines the costs, but not the benefits, of government requirements. It recognizes that almost all government requirements are addressed to important social objectives, and that many in fact make a major contribution to achieving those objectives. At the same time, all government requirements impose costs. We are interested in studying and eventually reducing those costs so that the achievement of benefits will be as efficient as possible.

Second, this study examines costs as they are paid by businesses, that is, as the total impact of a number of requirements. The study attempts to identify and estimate cumulative impacts of all types of requirements from all levels of government as they affect individual small businesses, both in aggregate and in several broad industrial and size categories. Although the study identifies programs and agencies whose requirements impose costs, it does not attempt to assign costs to individual requirements, programs, or agencies. Other studies have tried to make these individual assignments, but generally have not tried to examine the total impact. Therefore, this study defers to such individual studies (many are listed in the bibliography) and concentrates on total impacts.

Third, this study examines businesses in Washington state, primarily in western Washington. One reason was obviously to minimize travel and related costs. A second reason was to confine the research to a single political jurisdiction that is in a position to respond to the problems we find and the potential solutions we identify.

Nonetheless, we feel that this study has implications for areas far from our remote corner of the United States. To begin with, Washington is in many respects a relatively typical state. According to *The Book of the States*, in the middle 1970s Washington was twenty-second in population, twenty-eighth in population density, seventeenth in personal income, and eighteenth in farm income.[2]

Even more to the point, information from other areas, gathered largely through federal hearings and our conversations with researchers in other states, suggests that the problems we uncover and attempt to quantify are well-nigh universal. We conclude that a study of Washington state is a good case study for the nation as a whole: our detailed examination of this single state should be a very reliable indicator of the kind of findings that would emerge from detailed examinations of other states as well.

Notes

1. See, for instance, Arlene Hershman, "The States Move in on Business," *Dun's Review*, III (January 1978):33-38.

2. Council of State Governments, *The Book of the States 1978-1979*, Vol. 22 (Lexington, Ky.: Council of State Governments, 1978), pp. 614, 614-638, 328, and 509, respectively.

2 Background

History

Neither government requirements nor small businesses are new, yet the problem of their relationship is particularly acute now. Government requirements have increased in number and impact. At the same time, the vulnerability of small businesses has increased because large businesses and government agencies offer alternative sources of employment and competitive sources of goods and services. Yet small businesses may be especially important as centers of independence and innovation in the face of pressures inherent in large organizations against such independence and innovation.[1] In addition, certain goods and services are currently provided almost exclusively by small businesses. Therefore, achieving the benefits of government requirements at as low cost to small business as possible is especially important now.

Previous Research

Even though the problem is not new, a review of the literature relevant to the subject of this book reveals no prior attempts to assess how *all* types of government regulation result in a *cumulative* cost to individual small businesses. Most previous work has focused on aggregate costs as opposed to individual company costs, on one level of government or one set of requirements as opposed to an overview of all levels of government and all types of requirements, on specific types of impacts as opposed to inclusive cumulative impacts, on all business rather than small businesses, and on the government point of view as opposed to the business point of view. (Appendix B discusses the hypotheses implied in these previous works in light of our study.)

In general, few published sources of data deal directly with the costs of government requirements to small businesses. The data that do exist are often in the form of "horror stories" describing specific instances of negative experiences and calling for a reduction in the number of government requirements. In addition, these stories usually pertain to one kind of firm in one specific industry. They do not discuss the effects of the same or similar requirements on other types of firms or industries, and they do not focus on small business in particular. Thus it is difficult to ascertain how representative such stories are.

Approach

This study is an attempt to describe government requirements from the point of view of someone who owns or manages a small business. An owner/manager cannot concentrate on any one requirement or any one level of government; he or she has to worry about all of them. In addition, the business will probably bear most of the costs of the requirements but will probably not reap most of the benefits. Therefore, a concern with all types of costs, from all types of requirements, is appropriate for this study.

The principal concerns of the project are as follows:

To identify the requirements that impose costs (by subject matter and agency).

To quantify those costs when possible.

To identify existing and proposed programs designed to reduce costs.

To develop guidelines that should make reforms more effective.

To suggest alternatives that meet those guidelines.

To involve as many as possible of the public and private groups that could eventually implement reforms suggested by the research.

The basic approach in this study is to use previous work and initial interviews to develop hypotheses, then to gather data and use them to refine the hypotheses. The most important of these initial hypotheses concerns the definition of a small business and the typology of the costs imposed by government requirements.

There are a number of ways to obtain data concerning the impacts of government requirements on small businesses. One could, for instance, examine in detail the impacts of all government requirements on a single business or very small industry, perhaps by monitoring the business or industry for a period of time. A major limitation of this approach is that selecting a single business may not give very much information about the impacts on business generally. For instance, not all businesses are affected by regulations to ensure water quality. Another approach would be to conduct an exhaustive survey of a large sample of businesses in order to determine the costs and other impacts of requirements. An obvious drawback of this approach is that large surveys are expensive. Moreover, given the rate of change of government regulations, the results of an exhaustive survey, which would necessarily take a long time to conduct, could be out of date by the time they became available.

The approach here is to combine these two, using three major sources of data: (1) small businesses themselves, (2) government agencies whose requirements apply to small businesses, and (3) associations of businesses. We obtained data from these sources by conducting relatively long interviews (1 hour or more) with some individuals from each group and by asking them to participate in a mail survey.

We chose a manageable number of firms (four to six) in a few industries (three to four) and conducted fourteen formal interviews, plus other discussions, with the owner/managers. These subjects for case studies were selected, with the advice of PSI members and others involved in the business community, so as to provide a range of the regulatory problems that small businesses face. Approximately fifty other interviews were conducted with researchers, regulators, and association executives.

These data were supplemented with the results of mail surveys. We were able to add the mail surveys because the Association of Washington Business (AWB) agreed to print and mail a questionnaire to its members (90 percent of whom are small businesses), and government agencies at the federal, state, and city levels (Federal Executive Board, Washington State Office of Small Business, City of Seattle Department of Community Development) were willing to distribute or help distribute a questionnaire to their levels of government. In no case did we seek to develop a body of statistical data with which to generalize about the "average" small business. Instead, we sought to find the limits of the *range* of impacts felt by small businesses.

Throughout phase I, the research team worked closely with a number of private organizations and government agencies in addition to PSI. Some of these relationships are diagrammed in figure 2-1. Not only did these relationships assist in the provision of information needed for the research phase of this project, they also laid the groundwork for working relationships in later phases.

In the private sector, the research received indispensable help from a number of organizations. Prominent among them were the AWB; the Independent Business Association; the Puget Sound Chambers of Commerce and individual chambers and associations, including the Seattle Chamber and the Puyallup Chamber; the National Electrical Contractors Association (Seattle); and the Northwest Food Processors Association.

Battelle also started working with government agencies very early in this project because these agencies are an important source of expertise and their cooperation is essential in reducing the costs of government requirements. Several offices at the federal, state, and local levels were helpful and informative. They include the regional offices of the Small Business Administration (SBA) and the Federal Executive Board, the State Department of Licensing, the State Department of Commerce and Economic Development, and the Seattle Department of Community Development.

Selected individuals from these and other groups became advisors who were consulted at a number of points in the project, including (1) the initial

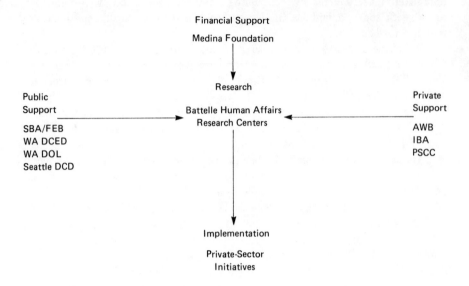

Figure 2-1. Organizational Support for the Small Business Project.

research design, (2) the selection of types of firms for case studies, (3) the development of questionnaires that were used for both case studies and mail surveys, and (4) the review of initial hypotheses. No advisor contributed input at every point listed; nonetheless, each made a significant contribution to the project.

Initial Hypotheses

Initial Definition of Small Business

The literature review revealed not only a proliferation of definitions of *small business*, but considerable controversy surrounding the subject. Numerous definitions have been proposed by government agencies, private organizations, and research studies. The most formal of these are the size standards of the SBA, which are generally based on number of employees or annual revenue. The SBA size standards vary from industry to industry and by type of eligibility (loan program, government procurement, and so on); they also tend to be much higher than those used in most other small business definitions. Other definitions include "enforcement thresholds" used by some government agencies, procurement limits set by individual states, membership definitions used by some associations, and size categories used by the U.S. Census Bureau and the Internal Revenue Service.

Obviously, most "official" definitions of *small business* are of more value for the administration of specific programs than for research purposes. This research needed a flexible definition that would reflect the particular difficulties small businesses have in bearing the costs of government requirements. We were interested in the crucial differences between small and large businesses that make the small ones less able to afford such costs. Therefore, for conceptual purposes, we defined a *small business* as one that is independently owned, has a single decision-making center, and is operated by an owner/manager who is the primary person to deal with government requirements. This definition corresponds in essence to the following one used in a major SBA report: "a small firm is one which does not benefit from the economies of scale under which large firms operate."[2]

Unfortunately, although this definition is appropriate for thinking about problems, it is not efficient for data analysis. Therefore, we chose "fewer than 50 employees" as the definition of *small business* to use in this book. We selected this version for several reasons. First, it is the official Washington state definition.[3] Second, it is the definition for which data could be obtained most efficiently. Obtaining data for other definitions would have required much more expense and time. We did use the SBA size standards in response to inquiries from larger companies about who should respond to our survey. Finally, all the definitions tend to be highly correlated with each other, so that a firm that is small by one definition is very apt to be small by the other definitions as well.

For all these reasons, an employment definition is appropriate in a research project designed to lead to public and private reforms. Some other definitions may still be appropriate for instituting these reforms; detailed design of particular reforms will almost certainly call for different definitions for different purposes. Having decided on an employment definition, we still investigated what definitions others use, especially the owner/managers of small businesses. We also examined the effect of using different employment limits in the quantitative analysis.

Definition of Costs

For the purposes of this study, we initially defined three general categories of costs imposed by government requirements. The first category is direct monetary costs related to licenses, fines, administrative inspections, record keeping, and the like. All firms must bear these costs of operation. However, economies of scale might tend to favor larger firms because such costs are usually not directly proportionate to size and large firms can develop specialized internal business components for managing these requirements. In a small business, these costs may seem relatively more important than they would in a larger one.

The second general category of costs is the time required for management to carry out compliance activities, to ensure that administrative inspections are conducted properly, and to keep abreast of requirement changes as they occur. The cost of an owner/manager's time to a small business in this instance is not merely a matter of salary. Perhaps the most precious resource of a small business is the expertise of the owner/manager and the top-level assistants. Any substantial diversion of that expertise into government-required activities is likely to have a relatively more serious impact on that business than would the same diversion if it occurred in a larger organization. The time spent by an owner/manager on government requirements is time subtracted from planning, marketing, and management of business operations. Depending on the amount of time denied such activities, government requirements may in some cases indirectly affect a small business's growth, profits, and general competitive posture vis-à-vis larger companies. As noted, managers of larger businesses hire staff to meet the administrative demands of government requirements. The fact that many small business owner/managers must become directly involved with government reporting, record keeping, and information gathering has the potential to create competitive disadvantages for small businesses.

The third major category of costs can be termed "trouble." These costs are the intangible burdens involved in compliance with government requirements; they may have the greatest impact on small businesses in ways not directly measurable by either time or money standards. Trouble may be manifest as the frustration, anxiety, bitterness, or depression that an owner/manager feels at being forced to comply with various types of government requirements. These intangible costs are based on the perceptions owner/managers have of government requirements and regulators; they affect how the owner/managers feel about their work. As such, these costs, though intangible, must be considered in any comprehensive assessment of the impacts of requirements on both the viability and efficiency of small business.

A major task of the research was to refine this initial definition of costs into a series of categories that could be identified and analyzed in individual businesses.

Other Initial Hypotheses

Most of the other initial hypotheses are related to why government requirements might have greater impacts on small businesses than on large ones. The major source of these hypotheses is a review of the previous literature in this field. The hypotheses are listed and discussed in appendix B. Basically, they are of two types: (1) those concerning various economies of scale such as occur in financing, administration, and political activity, and (2) those concerning the high desire for freedom from organizational restraint that is often an element in forming or maintaining a small business.

Notes

1. See Irving Kristol, "The New Forgotten Man," *Wall Street Journal*, November 13, 1975.
2. Charleswater Associates, Inc., *The Impact on Small Business Concerns of Government Regulations That Force Technological Change*. Final report prepared for U.S. Small Business Administration, Washington, D.C., September 1975.
3. Revised Code of Washington, Section 43.31.920.

3 Objectives

Major Goal

The goal of this research is to identify and analyze the impacts of government requirements on small businesses in enough detail to guide reform efforts. Such information should have several benefits.

First, this knowledge helps create interest in the plight of small businesses. The data could be used by sympathetic legislators to support their efforts to solve the problems. It could provide small businessmen with a better sense of their common difficulties and might make them more ready to work together toward solutions. For example, they and others in the private sector might seek changes in the requirements that affect them. An awareness by government agencies of the impacts of the requirements they administer could help induce those agencies to try to minimize the costs to small businesses. While Battelle cannot itself seek such changes, its research could be used by others for that purpose. There may well be common ground between the regulators and those who are regulated in improving the efficiency and effectiveness of regulations.

A second major benefit of such knowledge is that it could help steer further activity in this area. Using this information about the nature and amount of costs, future research could concentrate on the most severe and most avoidable costs. It should also provide clues to help identify and evaluate proposed methods for lessening those costs.

For instance, some small businesses experience great difficulty in identifying and understanding new requirements that affect them. They lack the administrative staff necessary to keep up with regulatory developments and to interpret them in relation to their operations as a whole. Although such problems may not be insurmountable for large corporations with sizable legal and other support staff, a firm that depends on a small general practice law firm and perhaps an accountant for advice in dealing with government may have great difficulty in complying with requirements in many areas.

A third major benefit of this research stems from the participants in it rather than from the data. The three-part team represents a new and important combination of resources. The example of a research organization, a business association, and a private foundation tackling the problem of small business and government requirements is apt to trigger further support, both governmental and private, for future activity.

Objective Sets

To reach the goal of obtaining information in "enough detail to guide reform efforts," it is necessary to achieve the following sets of objectives.

Objective Set 1

The objectives are to describe the small business population in Washington state and to answer these questions about it: What are the characteristics of small businesses that cause them to be affected differently by government requirements? How are these characteristics related to each other? What differences do they make? Which of these characteristics can form a basis for dividing businesses into "small" and "not small" for specific programs? The opinions of owner/managers are of particular interest in answering these questions.

Objective Set 2

The objectives are to identify, by subject matter and agency, the requirements that have significant impacts on small businesses. We are also interested in how the answers vary by level of government and by industry.

Objective Set 3

The objectives are to identify the types of costs created by government requirements, to quantify those costs where possible, and to convert quantities into dollar measures where possible. When quantification is not possible or reasonable, the objective is to provide a narrative description of the costs involved. The purpose is not to describe the "average" amount of impact so much as to identify the variation in impact across industries and individual firms.

Objective Set 4

The first objective is to identify as many as possible of the existing and proposed programs designed to reduce the costs of government requirements, especially those involving small businesses explicitly. These programs include both private and public ones at the federal, state, and local levels. The second objective is to identify the individuals and groups that are active in such programs or other reform efforts. Of particular interest are proposals for private-sector activity.

Objective Set 5

The objectives are to develop general guidelines for reform efforts based on the information obtained in achieving the first three sets of objectives just described, and to formulate suggestions that meet these guidelines. The primary source for these ideas is the information obtained in achieving the fourth set of objectives.

4 Methodology

Overview

Active research on this project started in late 1977 and proceeded throughout 1978. The tasks overlapped each other a great deal and did not always follow a sequential order. Figure 4-1 diagrams the rough chronological sequence of these activities, which were as follows.

Stage 1: Background Research (December 1977-April 1978)

Initially, extensive interviews were conducted with business and government representatives, researchers, and executives from a variety of associations. Then a review was made of published and otherwise obtainable articles, books, government reports, and previous studies related to government requirements on small business. And finally, the initial advisors were selected; that is, we developed a list of individuals (PSI members and others) who would provide advice at various points throughout the project. (This list changed over the course of the research.)

Stage 2: Development of Data-Gathering Techniques (March 1978-July 1978)

First, a search was made for a data base on the small business population of Washington state that best suited the needs of this research. Then, the kinds of firms to be used in case studies were selected. At this point, the specific information to gather was identified. We designed a questionnaire for use in the case studies and the mail survey. And finally, the advisors reviewed all of these tasks.

Stage 3: Data Gathering (June 1978-September 1978)

First, case study interviews were conducted. These were detailed interviews with selected small firms in various industries. Second, the small business survey was conducted. It included refinement of the previously-developed questionnaire, advisor review, pretesting, identification of potential respondents,

DEC.	JAN.	FEB.	MAR.	APR.	MAY	JUNE	JULY	AUG.	SEPT.	OCT.	NOV.	DEC.	JAN.

Lit. Acquisition/Review   Follow-Up

Initial Contacts   DC   Follow-up Contacts

Prepare & Hand
Out Project
Description   Progress Reports

         Small Business Survey
     Preparation   Circulation

         Case Study Interviews

         Government Survey
     Preparation   Circulation

         Association Survey
     Preparation   Circulation

         Data Analysis

         First Draft Report

         Comments

         Second Draft
         Report

         Comments

         Third Draft
         Report

         Comments

         Final
         Report

DEC.	JAN.	FEB.	MAR.	APR.	MAY	JUNE	JULY	AUG.	SEPT.	OCT.	NOV.	DEC.	JAN.

Figure 4-1. Work Schedule for the Small Business Project.

circulation, and tabulation of responses. Third, the government survey was carried out, again including development of a questionnaire, advisor review, pretesting, identification of potential respondents, circulation, and tabulation. And last, there was the association survey, with the same basic format.

Stage 4: Data Analysis (May 1978-September 1978)

Data analysis consisted of eight basic procedures:

1. Analysis of small business definitions (objective set 1).
2. Identification of agencies and programs that impose costs (objective set 2).
3. Refinement of the cost categories (objective set 3).
4. Analysis of costs by category (objective set 3).
5. Analysis of the government points of view (most objectives).
6. Analysis of the association points of view (most objectives).
7. Identification of programs to reduce costs (objective set 4).
8. Advisor review.

*Stage 5: Policy Implications (October 1978-
December 1978)*

In this stage, the general guidelines implied by the research were identified. Then a specific listing of suggested alternatives was made.

Stage 1: Background Research

Initial Interviews

Our first aim was to contact people with experience in the area under study. The goals of this process were to understand and define the problem and to identify individuals and organizations that might serve as ongoing sources of advice and assistance. To accomplish this, we conducted fifty-one interviews and contacted fifty-five additional sources of information. The interviews followed a standard format in which we asked participants to discuss three broad areas: the methodology of the study, the subject of the study, and any programs or reform efforts that address the issues under consideration.

Interview participants included federal, state, and local government personnel (both regulatory and assistance-oriented), association staff (including general business associations, trade associations, and Chambers of Commerce), and researchers (private, government, and academic). Most of the interviews took place within Washington state and Oregon. Some took place in Washington, D.C. with individuals at the national level. The people in Washington, D.C. were generally very supportive of the study's methodology and stressed the national value of "a study way out in the field, away from the Washington, D.C. atmosphere."

The interviews involved a large group of people in the project from the very beginning. Many of the contacts made in the first few months have provided valuable assistance throughout the study and will likely be instrumental in any subsequent proposal and implementation stages of the project. The even distribution of public and private individuals and groups contacted on both the national and regional level is especially valuable for future, more activist phases of the project.

Literature Review

The literature review was intended to identify previous research related to government requirements on small business and, in conjunction with the initial interviews, to define the parameters of the study. We first conducted a computer literature search, then supplemented it with general library research and discussions with academic and government researchers. The result was a preliminary bibliography, which was expanded throughout the study.

The types of literature reviewed include published articles (primarily in business, economic, and legal journals), U.S. government reports (especially reports of the Federal Paperwork Commission and the House and Senate Small Business Committees), contract research reports, related reports in other states, books on small business or regulation, and various unpublished materials (including drafts and appendices of major research reports, unpublished testimony before congressional committees, and so on).

Types of materials reviewed but not included in the bibliography are directories, federal regulations, Environmental Protection Agency and Department of Ecology economic impact analyses for various industries, relevant legislation, SBA management aid pamphlets, and standard statistical references on Washington state industries.

Several types of information were selected from the literature review to guide the design of the small business questionnaire. These include the following:

Definitions of small business.

Lists of agencies and requirements.

Data on national and Washington state small business populations.

Typologies of requirements.

Typologies of impacts.

Estimates of aggregate costs of requirements.

Estimates of cost and time for specific requirements.

Examples of impacts on specific companies or industries.

Hypotheses concerning the particular impacts of government requirements on small businesses versus large businesses.

Previous small business questionnaires—format and results.

The literature review also revealed a number of hypotheses others have made about why small businesses are affected by the costs of government requirements more than large businesses are. These are included in appendix B, along with some comments concerning their validity.

Advisor Review

During this period, we sent out several progress reports to PSI members and others, asking for comments on the research design in general and on the choice of interviews and case studies in particular. The response was generally supportive; it led to incorporation of approximately two dozen additional people into the group of those interviewed.

Stage 2: Development of Data-Gathering Techniques

Data on the Population of Small Businesses

One of the tasks of phase I was to assemble enough general information about small business to be able to estimate the good that would stem from reducing the impact of government requirements. Accordingly, a significant task early in the project was to find the best data for compiling information about small businesses in Washington state.

Three sources of data were considered for use in the study: (1) employment data from the Washington State Department of Employment Security, (2) tax and revenue data from the Washington State Department of Revenue, and (3) a special profile available through the Marketing Services Division of Dun and Bradstreet (D&B). A fourth candidate—custom data from the U.S. Census of Business—would have been considered if it had been available. Unfortunately, the Census data was not available in detailed form within the time and budget constraints of this project.

We chose the D&B data because D&B was the only source that included data by headquarters rather than by establishment. In determining the size of a business, we did not want to be misled by the size of individual plants if they all belonged to the same firm. The drawback to this method was that firms headquartered outside the state would not show up in this version of the D&B data, even if individual plants employed a sizable number of people and gathered a sizable amount of revenue within the state. This understatement is a less serious problem than the overstatement that would have resulted from using establishment data.

The D&B data show that 65,723 of the state's 69,050 private firms, or 95 percent, have fewer than fifty employees. (The state itself uses fifty employees as a cutoff measure for its small business programs.) Of the state's 1,213,261 employees, 394,690 work in firms with less than fifty employees. The distribution among major industrial divisions by number of firms and by number of employees is illustrated in figures 4-2 and 4-3.

A cursory look at data from the national level and from other states showed once again that Washington state should be an acceptable case study. Although the proportions of businesses in each of these categories do vary from state to state, Washington has enough businesses in each category to illustrate the kinds of problems likely to occur. In addition, nothing about the industrial or political patterns in Washington state suggests that the problems of small businesses would be particularly easy or difficult compared with other states.

Selection of the Kinds of Firms to Use in Case Studies

During this period, a tentative selection of the kinds of firms to use in the case studies was made. The major goal was to identify firms in a number of different industries that would have experienced various levels and kinds of impacts. At the same time, the industries chosen had to be "important" in some sense; therefore, the following data were examined (complete citations are in the bibliography):

1. The five growth areas in Washington state employment (*Job Opportunities Forecast*): service, retail, wholesale, finance, and self-employment.
2. The three highest "value-added" industries in Washington state (*Statistical Abstract*): transportation, lumber, and food.
3. The U.S. industries with highest percentage of sales, employees, and businesses in the "small" category (SBA Study II, Appendix): general building construction, special trade contractors, lumber and wood products, wholesale trade, retail trade, hotel/motel, personal services, repair services, auto shops/service stations, and amusement and recreation (not in order).
4. The percent distribution of Washington employment by industrial division for 1975 (*County Business Patterns*):

    Manufacturing   27.0%
    Services   21.7%
    Retail trade   21.6%

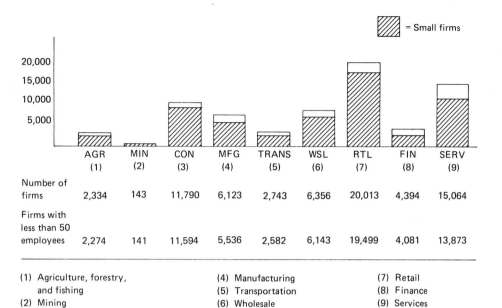

	AGR (1)	MIN (2)	CON (3)	MFG (4)	TRANS (5)	WSL (6)	RTL (7)	FIN (8)	SERV (9)
Number of firms	2,334	143	11,790	6,123	2,743	6,356	20,013	4,394	15,064
Firms with less than 50 employees	2,274	141	11,594	5,536	2,582	6,143	19,499	4,081	13,873

(1) Agriculture, forestry, and fishing
(2) Mining
(3) Construction
(4) Manufacturing
(5) Transportation
(6) Wholesale
(7) Retail
(8) Finance
(9) Services

Figure 4-2. Distribution of Washington State Businesses, by Industrial Division.

Wholesale trade	8.1%
Finance, and so on	7.4%
Transportation, and so on	6.4%
Construction	5.8%

5. The specific Washington industries with highest proportions of state employment for 1975 (*County Business Patterns*):

Health services	7.7%
Transportation equipment	7.1%
Eating and drinking places	6.3%
Lumber and wood products	4.4%
Auto shops/service stations	3.2%
Business services	3.0%
Food stores	3.0%
Miscellaneous retail	2.8%
General merchandise stores	2.7%
Special trade contractors	2.7%
Food and kindred products	2.7%

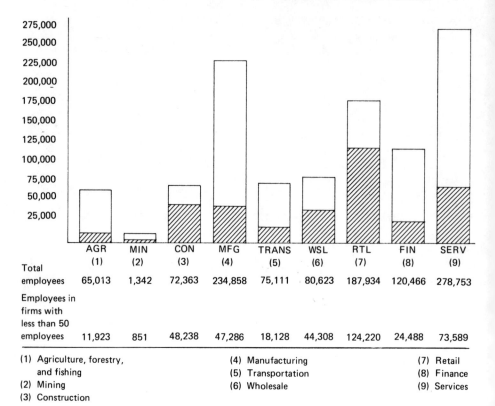

	AGR (1)	MIN (2)	CON (3)	MFG (4)	TRANS (5)	WSL (6)	RTL (7)	FIN (8)	SERV (9)
Total employees	65,013	1,342	72,363	234,858	75,111	80,623	187,934	120,466	278,753
Employees in firms with less than 50 employees	11,923	851	48,238	47,286	18,128	44,308	124,220	24,488	73,589

(1) Agriculture, forestry, and fishing	(4) Manufacturing	(7) Retail
(2) Mining	(5) Transportation	(8) Finance
(3) Construction	(6) Wholesale	(9) Services

Figure 4-3. Employees of Washington State Businesses, by Industrial Division, by Firm Size.

    Other important factors in the choice of industries were access to trade associations, integration into a "product chain," written resources on the industry, the industry's impact on marginal employment, and whether or not the industry was struggling for survival.

    The five industries selected for case studies were wood products, including sawmills, millwork factories, wholesale or retail lumber products, and homebuilding; food products, including food processors, food dealers, and restaurants; selected manufacturing, including smaller aerospace-related companies; selected services, including health services and the hotel/motel industry; and trucking.

Designation of Specific Information to Gather

The major goal of the first two stages of the research was to develop a theoretical and practical tool for identifying and estimating the costs of government requirements to individual small businesses. The tool developed was an extensive questionnaire that was later used both in the case studies and in a mail survey of small businesses. It also provided a basis for developing the questionnaires used in interviews and mail surveys with government personnel and association executives.

The questionnaire is extensive because it was intended to apply to a wide range of business types and sizes, as well as to a wide range of potential impacts, including both those which affect large numbers of businesses and those which affect small numbers in special cases.

The questionnaire was developed over a 3-month period, through approximately five drafts. It was pretested and reviewed by PSI members, other local contacts, contacts made in Washington, D.C. (with prior experience in small business questionnaires), academic consultants, and the Battelle staff (with experience in survey research).

The small business questionnaire is divided into eight major parts:

1. Company profile
2. Identification of agencies and types of requirements
3. Direct compliance costs
4. Administrative costs
5. Information and avoidance costs
6. Start-up costs
7. Opportunity costs
8. Cumulative impacts

These parts are discussed in detail in the following sections.

The small business questionnaire contains several types of question formats, including multiple choice, detailed matrices, cost tallies, and open-ended responses. The emphasis on closed-end and single-answer responses was intended to ensure consistency among responses and to reduce the amount of time necessary to respond to essential questions.

We were aware of the irony inherent in a "questionnaire on government requirements" and the length and complexity of this questionnaire compared with those normally used in mail surveys and case studies, but we felt that given the wide variation among firms, there was no other adequate means of estimating government impacts.

A major goal of the questionnaire was to provide small business owners with a framework within which to consider and categorize government-induced costs. The case-study interviews showed that small business owners and managers found the format of the questionnaire intuitively appealing and well adapted to expressing their experience with government requirements. One respondent wrote:

I am pleased that you are taking on the task of gathering factual information concerning the costs of government requirements particularly because it will point out the insidious nature of the multitude of requirements as they are stacked one upon the other on small business. (I am sure that the cost to large businesses is greater in number of dollars and energy wasted but as a percentage of business costs, it has to be greater for small business.) Your questionnaire has made me analyze more carefully how I spend my time and I can assure you that a significant portion of my time as chief executive officer is spent in government-related activities.

Although many respondents were supportive of the survey, some objected to filling out yet another questionnaire, especially one of such detail. For example, when asked which government reports took the most time, one small business owner wrote, "Ones like this one!" Another respondent noted in the margin that "this report in itself if completely researched is as bad as any of the government reports."

In general, both the quality and quantity of data received were good. However, certain qualifications should be made. First, there was a wide range of quality in individual responses. Time spent per questionnaire ranged from 5 to 10 minutes to several hours, with the maximum amount of time spent reported as 10 man-hours. Second, very few of the respondents reported that they maintained records of time or money spent on government inspections, reporting, record keeping, and so on. In fact, many stressed that figures they had reported were "guesstimates" only. However, a sufficient number of "guesstimates" in a particular industrial category should yield a fairly accurate composite picture of costs and impacts in that industry.

In terms of one of the basic objectives of the study—to *identify* the costs of government requirements to small business—the survey questionnaire is both a research tool and an accomplished end in itself. The breakdown of costs presented in the questionnaire represents a concise distillation of the literature, combined with experience obtained from the initial interviews and questionnaire pretesting. As a theoretical and practical tool for identifying costs and impacts, the small business questionnaire is a central accomplishment of this study. After completing it, one respondent asked:

Is it possible that the very complexity of this survey does not tell the story better than any of the answers? Would it be possible to force every bureaucrat and government employee to answer as many truly searching questions as you have? I pray it will all help.

Company Profile. An important objective of the study was to develop a definition of *small business* that reflects the particular problems such businesses face because of their size. The initial interviews and literature review revealed that this subject is characterized by confusion and controversy. To obtain detailed information from respondents to the small business survey concerning characteristics of their own businesses and their opinions regarding a definition, the following descriptive items were included in the questionnaire: number of employees; average annual revenue; business characteristics, including unionization, legal organization, geographic area served, affiliation with a larger corporation, and number of establishments; measurements of available expertise, including number of decision makers and support staff; and degree of access to legal and accounting expertise. This section concluded with questions asking respondents to indicate whether they considered their businesses small and to give their own definitions of a small business.

Identification of Agencies and Types of Requirements. Another of the study's objectives was to identify the government agencies that impose costs on small business and to specify the requirements that create these costs. A related objective was to assess the range of impacts on different types of industry. This information may be valuable to small businesses, government personnel, and associations in designing solutions to the problems identified in this book. As noted earlier, however, it is not the study's intention to single out specific agencies and requirements based on a limited number of subjective responses.

Two matrices included in the small business questionnaire were used to obtain this information. The first asks respondents to indicate whether or not government requirements in a number of areas affect their businesses,[1] which level of government administers the requirements, and whether the impacts are light, moderate, or heavy. The second matrix was intended as a cross-check of the first. Respondents are to indicate whether their businesses have had contact with specific federal agencies during the past year, the frequency and nature of the contacts, and whether the impacts are light, moderate, or heavy. Similar constructions were used for state and local agencies. The lists of agencies and types of contacts in the second matrix were developed based on information from the initial interviews and literature review. (Appendix A contains copies of the two matrices.)

Direct Compliance Costs. The next six sections of the questionnaire addressed each of the six major types of government-induced costs identified through the initial interviews and literature review. Direct compliance costs were the first category of the six. These include direct payments to the government in the form of license-related fees or disciplinary fines, direct costs of changes made to comply with government requirements, and administrative or employee costs relating specifically to the act of compliance.

Administrative Costs. These include the amount and type of personnel time spent on routine administrative processing of government inspections, reporting, applications, and record keeping. Important variables were amount of time and percent of total work time spent by type of personnel (that is, manager, bookkeeper, secretary, and so on), and percent of total administrative costs attributable to government reporting and record-keeping requirements. A comprehensive list of possible miscellaneous administrative costs was also provided in this section of the questionnaire. This section also attempted to identify duplicative requirements and any "bunching" of reporting requirements that could create unnecessary additional costs.

Six primary variables were analyzed in the section relating to administrative costs. These variables included hours per year for inspections, hours per year for government-related record keeping, percent of owner/manager's time spent on government reporting and record keeping, percent of total administrative costs related to government reporting and record keeping, and miscellaneous administrative costs.

Together, these figures could help to generate a rough estimate of government-related administrative costs for a particular size business in an individual industry. The figures on time spent and the figures on percent of time or cost could also be compared for selected industries.

The analysis in this section dealt primarily with distribution of median hours, percentages, and costs for the six major divisions. The figures generated by this analysis should not be interpreted too literally; however, they are indicative of general tendencies among respondents in the six divisions. It should also be noted that the relative distribution of administrative costs may have more to do with business size than business type.

Another important qualification concerning the data on administrative costs relates to the inclusion of tax-related reporting and record keeping by some businesses, in spite of the proviso in the questionnaire instructing the respondent *not* to include tax forms. Responses often varied widely for similar businesses, depending on whether tax-related costs were included. This problem might be alleviated by eliminating the high range of responses, or by separately estimating tax-related expenses and subtracting from the high range of responses. For the purposes of the present analysis, all administrative cost figures are presented in their original form. Although the medians might be slightly lower without the inclusion of tax-related expenses, the comparative distribution should remain basically the same, with the possible exception of retail and service industries, which displayed more of a tendency to include tax-related reporting and record keeping in administrative cost responses.

Information and Avoidance Costs. Information costs include the money, time, and trouble involved in trying to understand what is required by government. Questions on information costs evaluated the type and quality of information available to the small business owner/manager, the ability to understand what is required, and the need for outside expertise. Avoidance costs represent the time and money spent in challenging or avoiding government requirements.[2]

Questions on avoidance costs dealt specifically with challenges to government actions.

Information and avoidance costs involve both tangible and intangible impacts on a small business. Tangible information costs include annual costs of subscription services, association memberships, managerial or staff research time, and legal fees. Tangible avoidance costs include contributions of time or money to political activity, costs of managerial or staff time spent in challenging a government ruling, legal fees, plus whatever aspects of information gathering are directly related to challenging or avoiding government actions.

Intangible costs of information and avoidance stem from process issues, such as the small business owner/manager's relationship with government, which are discussed in the subsection entitled Cumulative Impacts.

The tangible costs of information and avoidance are theoretically "voluntary" in the sense that they are not specifically mandated by government. However, seeking information and challenging government actions may be necessary adaptations to government requirements, to the extent that government fails to provide adequate information or makes an error in some aspect of enforcement. Tangible costs of information on requirements are also influenced by the intangible costs associated with an owner/manager's relationship with government. For example, a lack of faith in government information or actions may lead to higher "voluntary" expenditures on information and avoidance, as an adaptive response to problems in that relationship.

Start-Up Costs. This category of costs represents an attempt to evaluate observations made in the initial interviews that prohibitive barriers to entry may be caused by government requirements in some industries. Of course, we could only study the survivors of this process. We could not study the "invisible victims," that is, businesses that never begin or businesses that make up the high failure rate among new small businesses. The subcategories of cost include all the other cost categories (such as direct compliance costs, administrative costs, and the like) when those costs occur *before* the business is operating or at the very beginning of its operation.

Opportunity Costs. This category of costs includes those business activities which are avoided, delayed, curtailed, or discontinued as a result of government action or inaction. The types of activities listed are those most frequently identified in the literature and initial interviews as being avoided or otherwise impaired by government delay, complexity of requirements, cost of requirements, or uncertainty of requirements. These activities include construction or rental of additional plants or offices, hiring of additional employees, expansion of product lines or services, product development, expansion into new geographic markets, application for work under government contract, change in location, and property development. Opportunity costs are potentially higher than most direct, administrative, or other tangible short-term costs of government requirements. They primarily involve potential additional income (and consequently additional employees) foregone because of perceived or actual impacts of government requirements.

Cumulative Impacts. A category of costs called *cumulative impacts* was included at the end of the questionnaire to address the larger impacts of government requirements on various aspects of small business operations, including price of goods and services, quality of goods and services, location of business, business growth, business profits, competitive position, innovation, employment, and relationship with employees.

In addition, there were three categories which might be called *psychological costs*: relationship with government, managerial independence, and "enjoyment" of doing business. Responses to these attitudinal questions often displayed a "fervor" which did not seem justified by responses in the various cost categories throughout the questionnaire. One respondent commented on this discrepancy in his own questionnaire:

> I was surprised when filling out the questionnaire that I did not rate very many government agencies as having a major effect on our business. This did not correspond with my negative feelings concerning the entire government-business relationship . . . [and my feelings] concerning cumulative impacts. It really emphasized the true nature of government regulations and requirements on small business.

These psychological costs associated primarily with the business/government relationship seem to exert an influence on each aspect of the day-to-day relationship between business and government, often tending to exaggerate the impact of individual requirements, even those which by themselves are not particularly burdensome.

Advisor Review

As mentioned before, the list of data to gather was in the form of a questionnaire used in the case studies and mail survey. Before the questionnaire was used, however, three major kinds of review took place. The first was conducted by some of the knowledgeable individuals who advised us throughout the project. For example, Bill Robinson and Doug Marshall from AWB made particularly extensive comments. In addition, other useful comments were received from individuals in Washington, D.C. who had been involved in previous mail surveys of small business. The second kind of review came from people experienced in questionnaire preparation. The most extensive comments were made by a Battelle sociologist with experience in survey research. The third kind of review came from small business owner/managers in the form of five pretests of the questionnaire.

The reviews showed that the questionnaire did address the right issues in the right form, but was longer and more detailed than usual for a mail survey. At the same time, most of the advisors agreed that its length and complexity accurately mirrored the characteristics of the problem. Therefore, we made some question-by-question changes that were suggested (the questionnaire went through five drafts), but did not shorten it. For the study's purposes, detailed responses from a smaller proportion of businesses are more valuable than much more general responses from a larger proportion.

Detail was more important than response rate for two reasons. First, we were trying to determine the range of responses rather than the "average" response. The length and complexity were necessary in order to identify extreme cases. Second, we were asking questions whose answers stemmed in a calculable way from the situation in which the business answering the questions was involved. Therefore, if the kinds of businesses answering the questions matched the general population of small businesses, the answers were very likely representative, even if the percentage response rates were low. This situation *was not* like that of attitude surveys, where attitudes have little or no calculable relationship with more "objective" measures such as the age and sex of those responding. Although a match between the surveyed population and the total population on nonsurvey items is no guarantee of anything in attitude surveys, it was a supportive factor in this cost-calculation survey.

Stage 3: Data Gathering

Data for analysis came from three major sources: (1) small businesses in Washington state, (2) government agencies whose requirements apply to small businesses, and (3) associations of businesses. We conducted relatively long interviews (1 hour or more) with individuals from each group and conducted a mail survey of each group. The interviews with individuals from government agencies and associations were part of the initial interviews already discussed; the interviews with individuals in small businesses are the case studies described next.

Case Studies

Case study interviews of individual small business owner/managers were used to cross-check and detail the results of the small business questionnaire, to generate illustrative examples of types of costs, and to offer the study a basic check of the reality in the field.

We conducted fourteen case study interviews over a 3-month period. Initially, businesses were identified through individual trade associations, the

Puget Sound Chambers of Commerce, and the respondent group of the small business questionnaire. Two basic approaches were used in the interviews. The first approach, which did not prove to be significantly more useful than the mail questionnaire, consisted of an on-site (first visit) duplication of information requested in the questionnaire. The second approach, which proved far more successful, involved a detailed follow-up on an already completed questionnaire. Summaries of eight case study interviews using this latter approach are presented in appendix C. The others are not summarized because they yielded essentially the same information as the questionnaire.

In addition to asking follow-up questions on individual responses, we sought information on the administrative framework that each business had evolved in response to government requirements. Another important emphasis of the case study interviews was to ascertain the attitudes of owner/managers toward government or regarding government requirements affecting their businesses. We also sought more detail concerning sources of information available to the owner/managers. Industrial categories of the fourteen case study interviews to date are as follows:

Wholesale growing nursery (SIC 01)

Homebuilder (SIC 15)

Electrical contractor (SIC 17)

Glass installation and service company (SIC 17)

Fruit processor (SIC 20)

Wood products manufacturer (SIC 24)

Custom millwork shop (SIC 24)

Chemical manufacturer (SIC 28)

Electronic equipment manufacturer (SIC 36)

Trucking company (SIC 42)

Moving and storage company (SIC 36)

Engine parts wholesaler (SIC 50)

Retail heating oil companies and services stations (SIC 59)

Photographic lab (SIC 73)

Mail Survey of Small Businesses

The mail survey was an attempt to solicit data from sources additional to those reached through the case studies. We used the questionnaire described earlier.

The bulk of the questionnaire mailing was made possible by support from the AWB, which absorbed costs for printing and mailing the questionnaire to its members (3,002). Additional questionnaires were circulated by the Independent Business Association (200 questionnaires), Puget Sound Chambers of Commerce (identification of over 200 businesses), and other sources, including the Puyallup Chamber of Commerce and the Seattle chapter of the National Electrical Contractors Association. (A complete copy of the questionnaire is provided in appendix A.)

As a consequence, only small businesses with membership in a business association or a Chamber of Commerce received copies of the questionnaire (in the case of the Independent Business Association and the Puget Sound Chambers of Commerce, questionnaires were sent to those businesses "most likely to respond"). This might tend to select businesses with a higher-than-average concern and awareness about government requirements. Nonetheless, the businesses sent questionnaires resembled the general population of businesses in other characteristics (type of industry, size, and so on).

From the circulation of approximately 3,500 questionnaires, we received almost 400 replies; 360 of the replies were suitable for coding and analysis. This response rate of approximately 11 percent may seem low in comparison with response rates of 50 percent or better reported in other mailback surveys, but it is not low in this context. First, the questionnaire was particularly long and complex. Second, the 50 percent response rate achieved in other surveys came only after extensive follow-up (second and third mailings, calls, and so on) that would have been outside the resources of this project. Third, two other questionnaires to small businesses, much shorter and simpler, got roughly 16 percent response rates: Charleswater Associates (see bibliography for complete reference), 2,900 questionnaires mailed, 469 returned; and Peat, Marwick, Mitchell and Company, 1,008 firms, 162 responses. In the second case, local offices of Peat, Marwick, Mitchell and Company did do follow-up to encourage response. Fourth, respondents in this study were similar to the general population of small businesses (see subsequent discussion). In this context, similarity is a good sign, as the subsection entitled Advisor Review has already discussed.

Finally, we were not seeking to represent all small businesses, in the sense of conclusively identifying the average or "typical" costs. (In statistical terms, we did not try to put validly narrow confidence limits on various measures of central tendency.) Instead, we sought to determine a range of costs, to rank various types of costs, and to show how costs could be estimated for individual companies with widely different types of impact.

The questionnaires were processed by computer, using the Statistical Package for the Social Sciences (SPSS). Because the mail survey results and the case study results reinforced each other, the survey results are used to describe the findings.

The distribution of respondents by major industrial division is similar to the distribution of Washington state businesses with less than fifty employees, as illustrated in figure 4-4. The differences are not large enough to be statistically significant (according to the Chi-square test at either the 0.05 or 0.01 levels of significance).

The sample differs from the actual distribution of firms primarily in a higher proportion of manufacturing respondents. This result, as well as lesser discrepancies between the distributions in construction, retail, services, and finance industries, can be accounted for by the slight tendency of the groups we sent the questionnaire to be weighted in the same direction. Firms from heavily impacted industry groups were more likely to respond.

The median firm in our sample had fifteen employees and an annual gross revenue of approximately $1 million. The relationship between respondent size and industry is important to remember when evaluating data from the small business questionnaire; that is, what may appear to be an industry-specific type of impact may actually be associated more closely with size, and vice versa (especially relevant in manufacturing). (See appendix D for a more detailed analysis of the characteristics of respondents.) Those businesses which responded to the questionnaire may have had a natural interest in doing so if they were more heavily affected by government requirements than other businesses were. This may be true to an extent, but certain countervailing tendencies make this kind of self-selection less pronounced. A large number of questionnaires were returned with many blank responses or reports of minimal impact in non-tax-related areas. It may have been easier for those firms which were normally not burdened by an inordinate amount of paperwork to respond. Also, those companies which were generally less affected would naturally find the task of filling out the questionnaire far less time-consuming than those with numerous and complex contacts with government.

Finally, after comparing the questionnaire data with data from the initial interviews, literature review, and questionnaires to associations and government agencies, we concluded that the small business questionnaire respondents were somewhat atypical in two related aspects of their behavior. First, respondents may have been more activist than the norm: 40 percent of all respondents reported having challenged or appealed a government ruling or proposed regulation affecting their business (which would appear to contradict an observation made in the initial interviews that small businesses were generally passive politically). Second, a significant minority of respondents exhibited a high degree of disillusionment and hostility toward government. It was not possible to determine from the data whether our sample was somewhat biased through self-selection toward businesses with a sizable psychological cost resulting from government requirements or whether it represented the attitude of the broader small business community. One advisor thought any difference between respondents and the general population represented additional knowledge of government on the part of the respondents. He thought the other firms would become just as disillusioned over time, if they were not already.

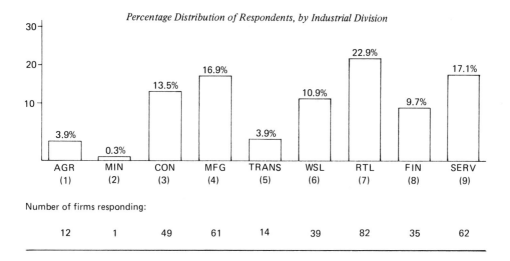

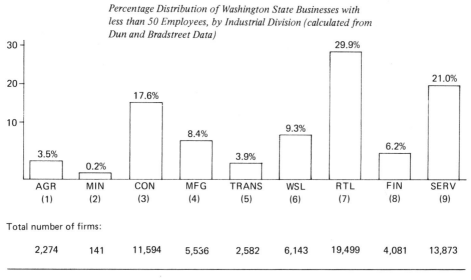

Figure 4-4. Comparison of Respondent Distribution with Distribution of Washington State Small Businesses.

Mail Survey of Government Agencies

The government questionnaire was developed concurrently with the small business questionnaire in an effort to gather similar data on requirements and costs "from the top down," and to give government personnel an opportunity for input in what could otherwise have been a relatively one-sided data base.

Questionnaires were mailed from the Seattle Federal Executive Board (with the help of the regional office of the SBA) to all federal regional and district offices, through the Small Business Office of the Department of Commerce and Economic Development (under Battelle cover) to twenty-seven selected state agencies, and from the Economic Development Division of the Seattle Department of Community Development to fifteen city departments. License-related information at the state level was provided by the Business License Center of the Department of Licensing. In all, fifty-two questionnaires were returned with a majority of state and local agencies responding. The questionnaire is included in appendix A.

Mail Survey of Associations of Businesses

The association questionnaire was designed to assess the information and advocacy services provided in relation to government requirements by Washington state associations and chambers of commerce. The need for this assessment was suggested by the observation in early case studies and interviews that small businesses lack accurate information about government requirements and are highly dependent on their associations for the information they do receive.

The association executives were asked to describe the methods their organizations used to gather and disseminate information about government requirements. We also asked for their assessments of the costs of government requirements to their memberships. This was intended to cross-check information obtained for specific industries in the small business questionnaire. In their role as association representatives, these executives might possess an overall grasp of requirements and costs within particular industries. In addition, we asked respondents for their ideas concerning methods for improving the current system.

A total of more than 500 questionnaires were mailed (350+ associations and 150+ chambers), with a response rate of approximately 17 percent. Associations and chambers were canvassed through a mailing list compiled from *Business Associations in Washington State*[3] and from a listing of chambers of commerce and associations provided by the Association of Washington Business. (See appendix A for the trade association questionnaire.)

Once again, the responses were consistent with the information obtained through the relevant initial interviews.

Stage 4: Data Analysis

The data gathered were used to achieve the objectives set forth in chapter 3. Specifically, they were analyzed along the following lines:

1. Definitions of small business
2. The agencies and programs that impose costs
3. Refinement of the cost categories
4. The costs within those categories
5. Programs to reduce costs
6. Government points of view
7. Association points of view

At this point, the focus was on findings of fact rather than on policy implications, which were discussed at a later stage. The results were published in a draft report and circulated for review by PSI members and other advisors. The comments these people made shaped not only the final version of these findings, but also the subsequent identification of policy implications.

Stage 5: Policy Implications

Identification of policy implications was not a straightforward task. In general, this kind of analysis demands that one go beyond the data available because policy implications are not calculable or deducible from data alone. Instead, such implications depend on value judgments and imagination, involving legal, organizational, and political knowledge and sensitivities outside the data at hand.

In this phase, we were looking for implications to guide phase II of the overall small business project. We wanted two kinds of guidance in designing and proposing reform measures to reduce the costs imposed by government requirements. The first was general advice about the conduct of reform efforts. We wanted to know what the data implied about the style and content of all reform efforts in this area. The second was specific measures that appeared to be worthy of further investigation in phase II. We wanted to compile a list of such measures so that phase II would have specific targets for its design and proposal efforts.

Notes

1. The areas were condensed from a typology of government actions developed in Bruce W. Cone et al., *An Analysis of Federal Incentives Used To Stimulate Energy Production*, Battelle PNL-2410, March 1978, available from NTIS, esp. pp. 35-44.

2. The term *avoidance costs* is adapted from a working paper done for the Center for the Study of American Business by Roland N. McKean, entitled "Avoidance and Enforcement Costs in Government Regulation" (1976).

3. Washington Department of Commerce and Economic Development, October 1977.

5 Findings of Fact: Part I

Overview

This chapter, and the next two, report the findings of the data-collection effort. Chapters 5 and 6 are divided into sections that parallel those used in the questionnaire. The final section of chapter 6 is a summary of costs by category, so readers who are interested only in highlights can go immediately to on to the section Digests of Costs by Category. Chapter 7 discusses findings that relate to more than individual sections of the questionnaire.

Owner/Manager Views of Definitions of Small Business

We asked respondents to comment on the following types of definitions: the basic elements of employment and revenue; business characteristics involving unionization, legal organization, geographic area served, affiliation with a larger corporation, and number of establishments; and various measures of available expertise, including number of decisionmakers (managerial expertise), and access to legal and accounting expertise. We concluded with an open-ended question asking for the respondent's own definition of *small business*.

Ninety-five percent of respondents (question A12) considered their companies to be small businesses. The seventeen respondents who did *not* consider their companies to be small account for most of the extreme high range in the questions relating to employment size and revenue size.

We decided to tabulate responses to question A12 ("How would you define a 'small business' in your industry?") by type of definition, rather than by specific definition. Specific definitions were for the most part simple restatements of some aspect of the respondent company's own size—either by picking a range slightly higher than their own size (for example, a "twenty employees" definition for a company with eighteen employees) or by describing a business characteristic based on their own company (for example, "family-owned business" or "local service"). This observation can be extrapolated to the hypothesis that if it were up to the small businesses themselves, official definitions would include almost any business that wanted to be considered small. For all respondents who considered their businesses small, the most popular definition (32 percent) was one based on annual gross revenue. Rankings of responses by type of definition are listed in table 5-1.

Table 5-1
Choices among Types of Definitions for a Small Business

Definition based on annual revenue	32.0%
Definition based on number of employees	23.0%
Definition based on business characteristics	14.0%
Definition based on industry characteristics	12.0%
Definition using a combination of revenue and number of employees	10.0%
Definition based on geographic area served	2.0%
Definition based on company assets	0.5%
Miscellaneous other types of definitions	6.5%

The most common federal definitions, based on employment size, revenue size, or a combination of the two, comprise 65 percent of respondent definitions, although most estimates were far below federal standards and emphasized revenue rather than employment. Definitions based on business characteristics included such diverse criteria as type of legal organization, number of establishments, number of managerial personnel, degree of affiliation with a larger company, and so on. Definitions based on industry characteristics generally involved number of units produced, serviced, or maintained or variations on other types of definitions applied specifically to the industry. Miscellaneous other definitions often referred to a relation to some government program or to access to various areas of expertise (for example, too small to afford data processing).

Comparisons between type of definitions tabulated for all respondents and those tabulated for respondents in separate industrial divisions reveal significant preferences which may be useful in devising future government definitions. Preferences by major industrial division are presented in table 5-2.

The most notable aspect of this distribution of responses by industrial division is that the preferred types of definitions tended to coincide with types of SBA standards for each industrial division (although the *range* of SBA standards is consistently higher). The marked predominance of revenue definitions in the construction industry is mirrored in the SBA standards.

Manufacturing, which tallied the highest percentage of responses for employment definitions among industrial divisions, is defined by the SBA strictly in terms of employment. (Revenue definitions also predominated in manufacturing, but only by a slight margin. It is also of interest that almost 60 percent of manufacturers chose definitions within the first three categories.)

Wholesale trade responses, also primarily defined in terms of revenue and employment, exhibited the smallest margin between employee and revenue definitions and contained the highest percentage of responses in the combination category of employees and revenue. These tendencies are reflected in SBA standards, which set a revenue limit for loans and an employee limit for

Table 5-2

Choices among Types of Small Business Definitions, by Industrial Division

Type of Definition	Emp.	Rev.	Emp./Rev.	Assts.	Area	Bus.	Ind.	Other	(Not Small)
All businesses	22.1%	30.0%	9.1%	0.3%	1.5%	13.3%	11.8%	6.7%	5.2%
Construction	19.1%	46.8%	10.6%	–	2.1%	10.6%	6.4%	2.1%	2.1%
Manufacturing	33.9%	35.7%	12.5%	–	–	3.6%	1.8%	7.1%	5.4%
Wholesale	19.4%	22.2%	16.7%	–	–	13.9%	13.9%	11.1%	2.8%
Retail	13.9%	36.1%	4.2%	–	–	29.2%	6.9%	6.9%	2.8%
Finance	18.2%	24.2%	6.1%	3.0%	9.1%	6.1%	12.1%	6.1%	15.2%
Services	31.0%	13.8%	5.2%	–	1.7%	10.3%	25.9%	5.2%	6.9%

procurement. Wholesale trade responses also contained a high range of responses for the definitions based on business and industry characteristics.

Respondents in retail trade showed a strong preference for revenue and business characteristic definitions. SBA definitions for retail trade are based on revenue for loans and employment size for procurement.

Respondents in the finance divisions (primarily banks, insurance agents, and real estate brokers) showed a preference for revenue definitions and also had the highest percentage of responses for the definitions based on assets (banks) and geographic area served. The SBA does not maintain size standards for the finance division.

Respondents in service industries represented the only dramatic departure from SBA standards, with a high predominance of definitions based on employment size. SBA size standards for service industries are based almost solely on revenue. The service division also showed the highest percentage of responses in the category of industry-specific definitions.

Definitions based on revenue were consistently favored by businesses with between five and ninety-nine employees. The smallest and largest businesses in our sample preferred definitions based on number of employees (0 to 4 employees, 34 percent; 100 to 249 employees, 33 percent).

Identification of Agencies and Types of Requirements

The major purpose of this section was to profile the regulatory framework within which the respondent company operated and to identify specific agencies and types of requirements with a notable impact on the company. However, as discussed in chapter 1, it was not our intention to single out specific agencies and requirements based on a limited number of subjective responses.

Results from this section indicated that businesses in the areas of construction, manufacturing, and wholesale were subject to more types of requirements, with relatively heavier impacts, than businesses in the areas of retail trade, finance, and services. Construction, manufacturing, and wholesale trade also tended to have more annual federal, state, and local agency contacts, with a heavier impact, than did the other industrial divisions. Median numbers of federal, state, and local agency contacts during the past year are presented in table 5-3.

Respondents often checked a larger number of applicable areas of requirements than corresponding agencies. The reasons for this tendency are unclear, but several explanations are suggested: (1) respondents realized that they were required to do something but could not specify which agency; (2) respondents realized that they were required to do something but were not contacted by the corresponding agency during the past year; and (3) the table for "areas of requirements" was easier to fill out than the table identifying specific agencies and types of contacts.

In general, smaller businesses listed fewer areas of requirements and fewer heavy or moderate impacts than did larger businesses. Both number of areas and impacts perceived increased steadily with business size (with a slight decrease for businesses with 100 to 249 employees). Likewise, the number of federal, state, and local agencies checked increased with business size, as did the number of heavy and moderate impacts linked to specific agencies.

A matching of specific industries and areas of requirements with heavy to moderate impact was possible in those SIC industrial categories where sufficient quantity and quality of responses were received. For example, respondents in lumber and wood products identified the areas of employee safety and health pensions, unemployment compensation, energy use and rates, and consumer or product safety as areas of requirements with heavy to moderate impact on their businesses (in descending ranking as reported by four to six respondents). Respondents in homebuilding, another industry in which this type of matching was possible, listed the areas of land-use/zoning, unemployment compensation, and solid-waste disposal.

Table 5-3
Median Number of Agencies Involved in Regulations, by Industrial Division

Industrial Division	Number of Federal Agencies	Number of State Agencies	Number of Local Agencies	Total Agencies
All businesses	2.0	3.1	1.6	6.7
Construction	3.0	4.3	2.2	9.5
Manufacturing	2.8	4.1	2.2	9.1
Wholesale	2.8	2.9	1.4	7.1
Retail	1.3	2.4	1.8	5.5
Finance	1.5	2.0	0.8	4.3
Services	1.5	2.9	1.4	5.8

An Example of Specific Agencies and Types
of Requirements

A tentative matching of specific industries and agencies (and types of requirements) with heavy to moderate reported impact was possible in those two-
digit SIC industrial categories where sufficient quantity and quality of responses
were received. An example of this type of matching of agencies and industries
is given in table 5-4 for homebuilding (construction) and lumber and wood
products (manufacturing) industries. Federal, state, and local agencies are listed
in descending order of impact ranking as reported by four to six respondents
in each industry.

Federal, State, and Local Impact Ranking

The responses to this question were fairly predictable, with 46 percent of all
businesses selecting a ranking of federal, state, and local and 26 percent selecting
a ranking of state, federal, and local. Although there was slightly more emphasis

Table 5-4
Matching of Industries and Agencies with Heavy to Moderate Impact
(Homebuilding and Lumber and Wood Products)

Agencies with Heavy to Moderate Impact		*Types of Requirements*
Lumber and Wood Products		
Federal	(OSHA)	Inspections/reports/orders
	Census	Reports
	EPA	Inspection/reports
	ICC, DOT, SBA	
State	WISHA	Inspections/reports/orders
	DOLI	Reports
	DOR	Reports
	HRC	Information/reports
	DES	Reports
Local	Fire	Inspections/orders/information
Homebuilding		
Federal	HUD (FHA)	Reports/inspections
State	DOLI	Reports
	DES	Reports
	DOL	Applications
	SMB	Applications
Local	Building	Applications/inspections
	Zoning	Applications
	Licensing	Applications
	Planning	Applications
	Fire	Applications/inspections
	Pollution	Applications/orders/inspections

on state or local in certain industries (construction, retail, and services), the federal, state, and local impact ranking proved to be consistent in each of the major industrial divisions. The only exception to the predominance of the federal, state, and local impact ranking was among the smallest businesses in our sample (zero to four employees), with 33 percent selecting a ranking of state, federal, and local. All responses listing the federal government as having the greatest impact (F-S-L, F-L-S, F) totaled 53 percent; all responses listing state government first (S-F-L,S-L-F, S) totaled 36 percent; and responses listing local government first (L-F-S, L-S-F, L) totaled 11 percent.

Reported Federal, State, and Local Agencies with Greatest Impact on Respondents' Businesses

One problem affecting the interpretation of this question was that between 30 and 50 percent of respondents listed the Internal Revenue Service as the federal agency with the greatest impact, although the IRS was not included in the accompanying list of federal agencies. This tendency to fail to distinguish between requirements and taxation also contributed to the high number of "votes" cast for the Department of Revenue in the state category (in tallying responses, the IRS was not included, while the Department of Revenue was).

We think the refusal to exclude the Internal Revenue Service and the area of taxation is highly significant. First, it shows that the small businessman does not distinguish between record keeping for tax purposes and record keeping for other purposes. Second, it suggests the extra antagonism (which also came out in our interview) reserved for tax collectors as opposed to other inspectors and regulators. As one person interviewed told us, "You would not believe how many small businessmen will spend two dollars to avoid paying one dollar in taxes." Third, it suggests that reforms designed to reduce the impact of government requirements will have to consider tax requirements, perhaps taxes as well, if they are to deal with the most troublesome contacts between government and business.

In the federal category, the Occupational Safety and Health Administration (OSHA) led all other responses (except the IRS, which was not coded) by a wide margin. But since OSHA has only an indirect jurisdiction in Washington state, this does not mean that the agency itself has a particularly high impact on small businesses. Two interpretations of this response are possible. First, a tendency noted in the case study interviews was that small business owners often identify a particular area of requirements with its corresponding federal agency, even though reporting and enforcement are administered on the state or local level. In this case, respondents may have been confused over the jurisdiction of OSHA versus the Industrial Safety and Health Division of the Department of Labor and Industries (WISHA).

A second possibility is that the responses to this question were more a function of "public opinion" than of careful consideration of impact. This interpretation is reinforced by the fact that OSHA also led responses in the retail industries, where WISHA impact would be expected to be minimal (WISHA received only one "vote" from retail businesses in the state government category). The percentage of all businesses that ranked a given federal agency as having the greatest impact appears in table 5-5. OSHA impact was reported highest in construction, manufacturing, retail, and services; "other" received the most responses in wholesale trade and finance; Bureau of Census responses were largely centered in retail services; Environmental Protection Agency (EPA), primarily in manufacturing; and Health, Education and Welfare (HEW), primarily in services. The federal agencies identified as having the greatest impact by industrial division are shown in table 5-6.

Table 5-5
Federal Agencies Identified as Having the Greatest
Impact (excluding IRS)

All Businesses (%)	
OSHA	28.3
Other	17.6
Census	11.2
EPA	7.5
HEW	5.9
EEOC	5.3
FTC	4.8
DOT	4.8

Table 5-6
Federal Agencies Identified as Having the Greatest Impact, by Industrial Division

Construction		Manufacturing		Wholesale		Retail		Finance		Services	
OSHA	12	OSHA	16	Other	4	OSHA	9	Other	9	OSHA	9
EEOC	3	EPA	4	OSHA	3	Census	9	FTC	3	Census	5
Other	3	Other	4	Census	3	Other	7	EPA	2	HEW	5
EPA	2	Census	3	FTC	2	DOT	4			EEOC	2
HEW	2	FTC	2	EEOC	2	FDA	2			Other	2
		SEC	2	FEA	2	FTC	2				
						HEW	2				
						SBA	2				

The percentage of all businesses that ranked a given state agency as having the greatest impact appears in table 5-7. Responses in the state category reflected the difficulty in distinguishing tax-related impacts from requirements. The state agencies identified as having the greatest impact by industrial division are shown in table 5-8. It can be inferred, however, that those industrial categories where the Department of Revenue (29 percent of total) was listed first (that is, wholesale, retail, and services) tended to be relatively less impacted by other state agencies. Construction responses identified the Department of Labor and Industries (may include WISHA) as having the greatest impact. WISHA ranked first among manufacturing responses, and most of the respondents in finance listed "other" agencies as having the greatest impact (primarily banking and insurance commissions).

The percentage of all businesses that ranked a given local agency as having the greatest impact appears in table 5-9. In the local category, building and fire

Table 5-7
State Agencies Identified as Having the Greatest Impact

All Businesses (%)	
DOR	28.9
DOLI	17.5
WISHA	16.3
Other	9.5
DOL	6.5
DES	3.8
WVTC	3.8
DOE	3.4
DSHS	3.4

Table 5-8
State Agencies Identified as Having the Greatest Impact, by Industrial Division

Construction		Manufacturing		Wholesale		Retail		Finance		Services	
DOLI	20	WISHA	21	DOR	15	DOR	24	Other	14	DOR	16
WISHA	9	DOR	12	DOE	4	DOLI	8	DOL	5	WISHA	8
DOR	6	DOLI	7	WISHA	3	DSHS	5			DOLI	6
DOL	3			DOR	2	Other	5			DES	3
				HRC	2	DOL	4			DSHS	3
				DES	2	AG	3			Other	3
				DOL	2	DES	2			DOE	2
						WVTC	2			DOL	2

Table 5-9
Local Agencies Identified as Having the Greatest Impact

All Businesses (%)	
Building	22.9
Fire	20.0
Other	14.3
Licensing	13.7
Planning	9.7
Zoning	5.1

departments were consistently identified as having the greatest impact on respondents' businesses, with the exception of finance, which identified planning departments as having the greatest impact (primarily real estate). Local licensing requirements also ranked high in services, retail, finance, and maufacturing.

There was little variation by size of business in agencies identified as having the greatest impact, except that identification of the Environmental Protection Agency, the Equal Employment Opportunity Commission, and the Industrial Safety and Health Division of the Washington DOLI was more prevalent among larger businesses.

Refinement of Cost Categories

The cost categories summarized in this section represent a distillation of the experience gained from the literature review, initial interviews, and questionnaire pretesting. The categories of cost were validated by the case studies and the mail survey as a tool for estimating the impact of government requirements on an individual small business. Our initial categories of time, money, and trouble are expanded in these more refined categories. In other words, a business will incur costs in the form of time, money, and trouble within each of these categories. In general, money is the most important factor in direct compliance and opportunity costs; time is most important in administrative and start-up costs; and trouble is most important in information and avoidance costs and cumulative impacts.

Direct compliance costs
    License/permit/registration fees
    Changes in work routines
    Changes in physical facilities
    Disciplinary fines

Administrative costs
   Inspections
   Reporting
   Record keeping
   Miscellaneous costs

Information and avoidance costs
   Cost of outside expertise (legal, accounting, association, subscription)
   Cost of staff time
   Cost of challenges

Start-up costs
   Direct compliance costs
   Administrative costs
   Information and avoidance costs

Opportunity costs
   Expansion
   Product development
   Relocation
   Government contract work

Cumulative Impacts on Business Operations
   Price of goods or services
   Quality of goods or services
   Location
   Growth
   Profits
   Competitive position
   Innovation
   Employment
   Relationship with employees

Psychological Costs
   Relationship with government
   Managerial independence
   Enjoyment of doing business

The categories just listed can be further broken down into directly mea-surable costs (direct compliance, administrative, information, and avoidance) and costs not directly measurable (start-up costs, opportunity costs, and cumulative impacts). Start-up costs are not directly measurable because their primary impact is in preventing business from starting.

Directly measurable costs can be divided among standard or expected costs, unexpected costs, and voluntary costs. *Standard or expected costs* include license, permit, and registration fees, administration costs, and basic information costs. In other words, they include costs incurred by all businesses to some extent every year. *Unexpected costs* include direct compliance costs such as changes in work routines, changes to physical facilities, and disciplinary fines. *Voluntary costs* include the costs of challenge to government actions and especially high information expenditures. In chapter 6, observations in each cost category are summarized.

Findings of Fact: Part 2

Analysis of Costs by Category

The first six sections of this chapter analyze the nature and amount of costs encountered in each of the refined cost categories listed in Refinement of Cost Categories in chapter 5. Following the sections on specific cost categories is a section that offers a general method for estimating the short-term costs of government requirements.

Direct Compliance Costs

Annual Cost of Licenses, Permits, Registrations, and Filings

Responses to this question ranged from zero to over $10,000, with a median response of approximately $200 per year. Businesses in construction, wholesale trade, and finance reported the highest costs in this category. Figure 6-1, which depicts the relevant data, is the first in a series in which we present data from questionnaire respondents by showing comparison with the median response by category. The center line represents the median for all respondents; the various points above and below the line represent median responses for each category listed. The distance from each median point to the center line is roughly proportional to the differences in median values indicated.

As figure 6-2 shows, our responses revealed no consistent pattern of licensing and other fees by size. We would expect this result, since most license fees differ little, if at all, from one size of business to another. The differences that do appear probably reflect the differing proportions of business types within each size category and the tendency for much larger firms to engage in more kinds of licensed activities.

Changes in Work Routines

Twenty-two percent of respondents reported changes in work routines to comply with government requirements, with the highest percentage of responses

Figure 6-1. Median Annual Costs for Licenses, Permits, Registrations, and Filings, by Industrial Division.

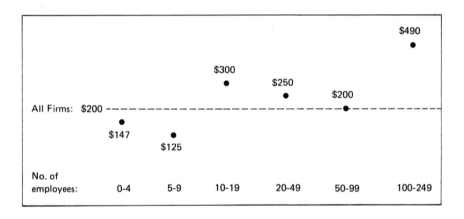

Figure 6-2. Median Annual Costs for Licenses, Permits, Registrations, and Filings, by Size of Firm.

falling in the construction (34 percent) and finance (22 percent) industries. Types of changes reported included hiring procedures, retraining programs, employee relations, and accounting procedures.

Reports of change in work routines increased steadily by size, as figure 6-3 shows. This result is not surprising (especially given the higher percentage of manufacturers in the higher size categories), but it does weaken a point suggested to us by several of the people interviewed—that smaller firms can usually change work routines more easily than larger firms. As a consequence, these people argue many smaller firms may prefer to meet requirements by

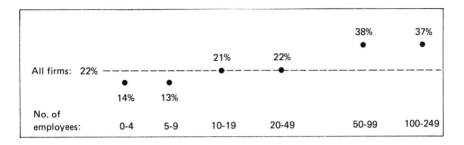

Figure 6-3. Percentage of Firms Required to Change Work Routines, by Size
of Firm.

changing work routines rather than by changing physical facilities. Our data
do not reject this point, but they do not support it either.

Changes to Physical Facilities

Thirty-two percent of respondents reported required changes to physical
facilities, with 16 percent reporting two or more required changes. A high 64
percent of manufacturers reported changes to physical facilities, with cost
estimates ranging up to several hundred thousand dollars. The median cost to
those who made physical changes was approximately $6,000.

As figure 6-4 shows, the percentage of firms required to make changes in
physical facilities increased with business size even more prominently than those
making changes in work routines.

Nonetheless, the percentages, both for work routines and for physical
changes, are high enough to suggest the pervasive impact of government. More
than one-fifth of all respondents, and more than one-third of the larger respondents, have had to make changes in work routines. Almost one-third of all
respondents, and more than half of the larger respondents, have had to make
changes in physical facilities. Our survey procedure was likely to select those
who were affected, but these results are consistent enough with other surveys
(cited previously) and our interviews to show, at the very least, that the direct
impacts of government requirements are not confined to a small number of firms.

Equal Opportunity and Affirmative Action

Responses to this section were slightly ambiguous, with a few respondents
(primarily in larger manufacturing, wholesale, and construction concerns)

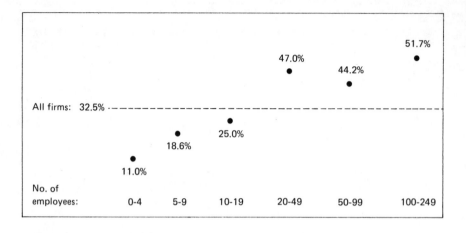

Figure 6-4. Percentage of Firms Required to Change Physical Facilities, by Size of Firm.

showing a definite impact and a large majority (58 to 82 percent) relatively unaffected. Among those respondents who indicated definite EEO-related impacts, there was a fairly even distribution of positive and negative appraisals of impact. Reports of EEO impact also increased with firm size. Firms with less than twenty employees generally reported minimal impact or no impact at all.

Disciplinary Fines

Fifteen percent of respondents reported having to pay any civil or criminal fines for alleged violations of government requirements, with most of the impact felt in the manufacturing and construction industries (31 and 20 percent of respondents, respectively). Of those businesses reporting fines, about one-third listed two or more fines since 1970.

Reports of disciplinary fines generally increased with business size. (In some cases, government agencies have adopted schedules to reflect business size.) However, as figure 6-5 shows, the smallest category (zero to four employees) contained a higher percentage than the next two categories. The data we have do not offer any satisfactory explanation for this result, although the smallest of firms also tend to be the least informed and thus most susceptible to enforcement actions.

Once again, our questionnaire was more likely to be answered by those involved with government in this and other ways than by those who had not been involved. Therefore, the percentages of all firms, as opposed to those firms

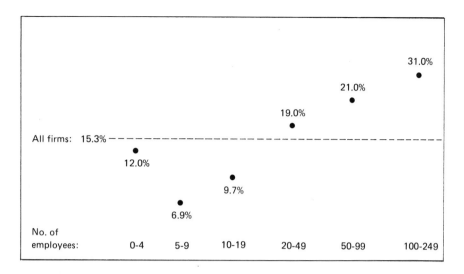

Figure 6-5. Percentage of Firms that Paid Disciplinary Fines, by Size of Firm.

which answered our questionnaire, are probably lower than these figures indicate. Still, these numbers are high enough, and consistent enough with other sources of data, to suggest a real problem. Being fined by the government is usually a relatively traumatic experience, even when the fine itself is low. All the firms involved with the government in this way are likely to have a much lower opinion of government and their relations with it as a result of the experience.

Administrative Costs

Inspections

Responses to "How many man-hours per year does your company spend on government inspections?" (question A) ranged from none (35 percent, primarily smaller companies in retail, finance, and services) to hundreds of hours. The median response for all businesses was 4.3 hours per year, with construction and manufacturing exhibiting the highest range, as figure 6-6 shows.

As figure 6-7 shows, the median hours spent per year on inspections increased with firm size, with one aberration. The general trend is not surprising. Our data do not suggest a ready explanation for the one difference in firms with 100 to 249 employees. In any case, the numbers are somewhat low, given that our sample is likely to consist of the firms more heavily inspected. Those low numbers suggest that complaints about inspections will stem more from the style of

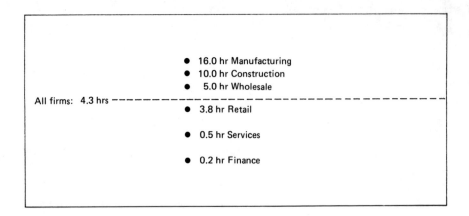

Figure 6-6. Median Hours Spent per Year on Inspections, by Industrial Division.

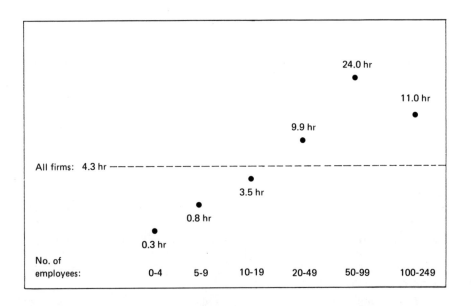

Figure 6-7. Median Hours Spent per Year on Inspections, by Size of Firm.

the inspection than from the actual time lost. Indeed, in a speech to a conference on OSHA, the lawyer for someone who took a case all the way to the Supreme Court to require OSHA to obtain a search warrant said his client had no particular quarrel with the inspection. His client objected to the manner in which the OSHA inspectors demanded admittance.

Responses to "Which inspections take the most time?" (question B) varied by industry. Some respondents listed "tax audits" in this category.

In a large majority of cases, the owner/manager of the business was identified as having responsibility for guiding or accompanying government inspectors (question C). In some larger businesses, this task was delegated to a foreman or plant or office manager. For most smaller companies, however, costs in the inspection category can be estimated by simply multiplying hours per year spent on inspection by a conservative estimate of the value of an hour of the owner/manager's time.

Reporting and Record Keeping

The most striking aspect of tabulated responses in this section was the extreme range of time spent, from 0 hours per year to several responses of over 1,000 hours per year for each category. As mentioned earlier this extreme range may be largely a product of which types of reporting and record keeping were included, with federal, state, and local tax reporting constituting a large share of the high range. In most cases, hours per year spent on applications (for licenses, permits, registrations, and filings) is a small percentage of the total reporting and applications figure. It is also unclear which routine types of reporting were included and which were omitted. For example, the 6 percent of respondents who spent 0 hours per year on reporting and applications clearly did not include tax reporting in their totals. However, it is unlikely that these respondents managed to avoid *all* other routine government reporting. Similarly, the 10 percent of respondents who spend 0 hours per year on government-related record keeping may be ruling out certain records that they would maintain with or without government requirements. Other businesses might operate with none of these routine records if not for periodic government reporting. But assuming a relatively consistent level of inconsistency among respondents, the distribution of median responses presented in figure 6-8 should resemble a hypothetical distribution generated by more consistent responses.

The distribution presented in figure 6-8 is fairly consistent with previous distributions involving the number of requirements of areas and the number of agency contracts by industry. A notable exception is wholesale trade, which lies much closer to the median number of hours for all businesses, even though respondents in wholesale firms listed far fewer than the overall median of agency contracts.

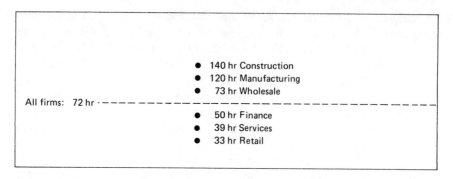

Figure 6-8. Median Hours per Year Spent on Reporting and Applications, by Industrial Division.

As figure 6-9 shows, the median number of hours spent on reporting increased with business size without exception. This result is consistent with our data from interviews, in which several people pointed out how the government actually discourages some employment because each additional employee represents a sizable addition to the amount of reporting required. This result is also consistent with the fact that many reporting requirements exempt small firms. For example, the Equal Employment Opportunity Commission has much more complete reporting requirements for firms with more than ninety-nine employees.

Since our case studies and responses to the questionnaire suggest that small firms often have no one other than the manager to fill out such forms, these figures suggest that at least some firms are losing from 3 days to a month of their manager's time per year simply to filling out forms. Here again, the likelihood that our sample contains more highly impacted firms prevents us from generalizing these figures statewide, but the figures do suggest how severe that impact can get.

The distribution of hours per year spent on government record keeping is parallel to the distribution for reporting, except that the relative positions of construction and manufacturing are reversed and the median figure for retail businesses is relatively much higher (possibly due to inclusion of sales tax records). In all industries, the median response for the time spent on government record keeping is higher than the figure for government reporting, as figure 6-10 shows.

As figure 6-11 shows, however, the hours spent on government-related record keeping do not appear to be a smooth function of the size of the firm. Our best explanation for this result is that smaller firms may be more likely to include tax records, while larger firms may be more likely to exclude them.

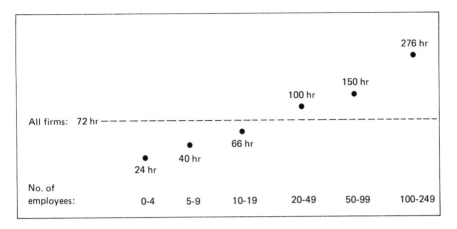

Figure 6-9. Median Hours per Year Spent on Reporting and Applications, by Size of Firm.

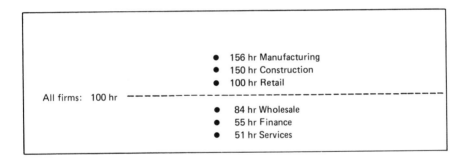

Figure 6-10. Median Hours per Year Spent on Government Record Keeping, by Industrial Division.

Therefore, we still believe the hours required are probably a relatively smooth function of size, even though the questionnaire data, as opposed to the interviews and previous studies, do not seem consistent with that conclusion.

Responses to "What percent of the owner's or chief manager's time is spent on government reporting and record keeping?" appear to be primarily dependent on business *size* in relation to total hours by industry group (see figure 6-12). The major effect of size on this response was the number of support staff available to the owner/manager and the degree of administrative staff specialization.

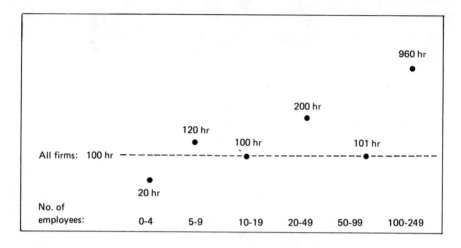

Figure 6-11. Median Hours per Year Spent on Government Record Keeping, by Size of Firm.

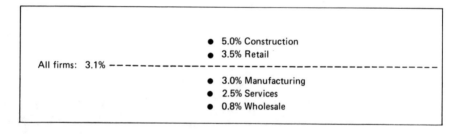

Figure 6-12. Median Percentage of Owner/Manager's Time Spent on Government Reporting and Record Keeping, by Industrial Division.

In the case study interviews, we discovered a variety of administrative mechanisms that had evolved in individual firms to handle government requirements. The following are examples of these administrative mechanisms in descending order of the extent to which the manager's time is involved:

The manager personally fills out all forms.

The manager handles any special reports and a bookkeeper handles routine reports.

The manager responds to difficult questions but relies on a secretary to handle routine questions.

The manager routinely routes government paperwork to a bookkeeper or assistant manager but reviews the documents before returning them to the government.

A personnel director who is a specialist on government requirements handles all the related tasks.

For example, although construction and manufacturing reported similar amounts of *time* spent per year, median *percentage* of manager's time spent was 66 percent higher for construction than for manufacturing. As noted in appendix D, the size distribution of manufacturing respondents is much higher than for respondents in construction (largely made up of small special trade contractors).

Small businesses in the construction industry reported the highest percentages of time spent by the owner/manager on reporting and record keeping. This is consistent with the overall high impact of government on the construction industry and the relatively small size of respondents in construction as compared with manufacturing.

One clear finding was that the amount of time spent directly by the owner/ manager on government-related administrative tasks was primarily dependent on business size. On one hand, the total amount of time required for reporting and record keeping increases steadily with business size. On the other hand, staff and administrative specialization available to relieve the owner/manager of routine paperwork also increases with business size. Thus the smaller the business, the greater the percentage of government-related administrative tasks the owner/manager must be responsible for. A theoretical model would predict that these two functions of business would interact as shown in figure 6-13.

When combined, these two functions represent the percentage of the owner/manager's total time spent on reporting and record keeping. The reported distribution of this variable by business size is consistent with the roughly bell-shaped curve predicted by the theoretical model.

Figure 6-14 shows the percentage of the owner/manager's time spent on government reporting and record keeping by size of firms. It appears that the very smallest firms are impacted the least, those in the middle range are impacted the most, and owner/managers of larger firms spend somewhat less time on reporting and record keeping. This pattern is consistent with, although not proof of, a theory that the smallest firms escape (or ignore) most government requirements, that the next sizes rely on the owner/manager to deal with government, and that the larger firms begin to assign people other than the owner/manager to deal with government.

As shown in figure 6-15, estimates of government reporting and record keeping as a percentage of administrative costs ranged from 0 to 90 percent, with a median of 5.1 percent. Distributions for this response vary according to total administrative costs (based on company size and industry) and total

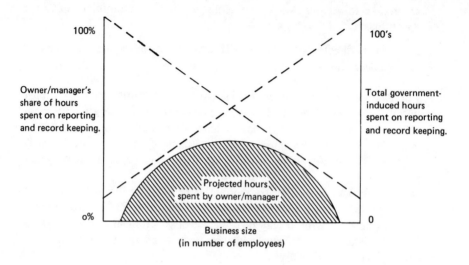

Figure 6-13. A Model of Owner/Manager Involvement in Government Reporting and Record Keeping.

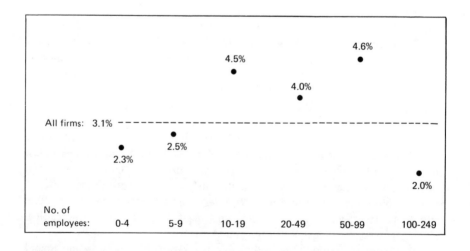

Figure 6-14. Median Percentage of Owner/Manager's Time Spent on Government Reporting and Record Keeping, by Size of Firm.

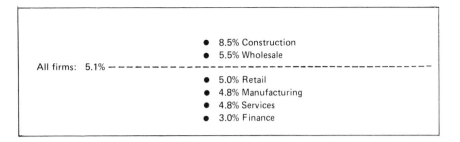

Figure 6-15. Median Percentage of Administrative Costs Spent on Government Reporting and Record Keeping, by Industrial Division.

hours spent per year on government reporting and record keeping. Median responses in this category are higher than those for percentage of owner/manager's time, with the exception of finance industries, where the median percentage of administrative costs is lower than the median percentage of owner/manager's time. In addition, the distribution of median responses for percentage of administrative costs is roughly parallel with the distribution for percentage of owner/manager's time, with the exception of wholesale industries.

Figure 6-16, which shows the percentage of administrative costs by size of firm, is consistent with, although not proof of, a theory that government requirements become a larger percentage of administrative costs as the firm size increases. In this case, we have to assume that the dip from ten to nineteen employees to twenty to forty-nine employees is simply an aberration of our sample.

Estimates of hours per year spent on reporting and record keeping can be translated into dollar figures by multiplying total hours by a conservative hourly wage estimate for the employee(s) responsible for government reporting and record keeping (question 2H). This figure can then be added to a cost estimate based on the percentage of the owner/manager's time spent on government reporting and record keeping (question 2I). The total of these two dollar amounts can then be compared with the percentage of administrative costs attributable to government requirements (question 2I). A cost estimate for this latter figure would be based on standard estimates of administrative cost as a percentage of annual revenue (question 6, part A) by industry (question 2, part A). A comparison of these two figures (hours per cost and percentage of adminstrative cost) would provide a high and low figure for an individual company's reporting and record-keeping costs attributable to government requirements. A composite profile by industry, size, or other variable would generate a high and a low cost range for government-related reporting and record keeping. (See the section in chapter 6 entitled A Method for Estimating Standard Annual Costs.)

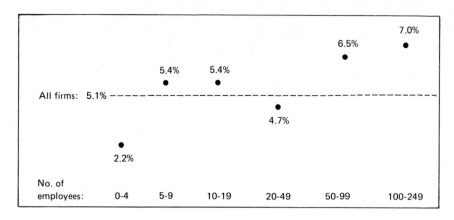

Figure 6-16. Median Percentage of Administrative Costs Spent on Government
Reporting and Record Keeping, by Size of Firm.

Miscellaneous Administrative Costs

Costs in this category included ancillary expenses associated with government
requirements, such as expenses for travel, duplicating, notary public, information distribution to employees, storage space for government-required records,
data processing, and overtime paid to employees (if government reporting
requirements are "bunched" at certain times of the year). Several of the case
study interviews confirmed the value of this category as comprising a portion
of those "hidden" overhead costs which are not readily traceable to government requirements.

The wide range of responses in this category (figure 6-17) appear to be
dependent on industry, business size, inclusion of tax reporting and record
keeping, and the method used to estimate costs (some respondents apparently
multiplied total costs in each category by percentage of administrative costs
attributable to government, while others used a zero-based approach to estimate
costs in each category). More than 40 percent of the respondents did not answer
this question. The distribution of median responses is given in figure 6-17.
The relative positions of manufacturing respondents and construction respondents in this figure may help to explain the high percentages of administrative and managerial time for the construction industry and also under-
score the size differential between manufacturing respondents and respondents in other industries.

Figure 6-18, which shows miscellaneous administrative costs by size of
firm, suggests that such costs may be a relatively smooth function of size of
the firm. Given what earlier figures have shown about hours devoted to reporting

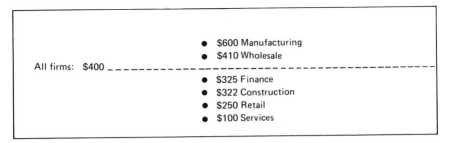

Figure 6-17. Median Annual Costs for Miscellaneous Administrative Costs, by
Industrial Division.

and record keeping, the result is no surprise. These expenses are part of the
"hidden total cost" of government requirements, but they are also highly
related to the less hidden costs.

An Example of Specific Sources of Costs

A tentative identification of specific sources of administrative costs was possible
in certain two-digit SIC industries where a sufficient quantity and quality of
responses were received. For example, table 6-1 shows the specific information
related to administrative costs reported by four to six respondents in lumber
and wood products (manufacturing) and homebuilding (construction).

Information and Avoidance Costs

Information Costs

Fifty-eight percent of all businesses in the survey responded negatively to the
question "Do you feel adequately informed about the nature and scope of
government requirements as they apply to your business?" The most uncertainty was displayed among wholesale (74 percent no) and manufacturing
(68 percent no) industries, while respondents in the finance and service sectors
felt adequately informed for the most part (75 and 57 percent yes, respectively). The differences among industries may be partially due to the relatively
higher number of agencies and requirements affecting manufacturing and wholesale industries (as identified in chapter 5). There does not appear to be a significant relation between size of business and feelings of being adequately informed.

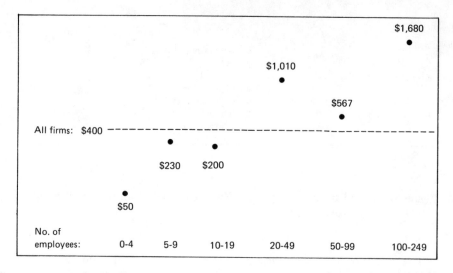

Figure 6-18. Median Annual Cost for Miscellaneous Administrative Costs, by Size of Firm.

Table 6-1
Specific Sources of Administrative Costs for Specific Industries

Question	Lumber and Wood Products	Homebuilding
Which inspections take the most time?		Local building department FHA
Which reports take the most time?	WISHA Census	Payroll taxes
Which licenses, permits, etc., take the most time?	HUD Corporate license Local building department	Building
Are any of your business activities regulated by more than one agency or government for the same purposes?	Profit sharing Environmental laws Excise taxes	Land use FHA and local building department DSHS and county health department

Most respondents rated the government information services provided by their associations as "excellent" or "adequate," and we also noted a strong tendency among businesses interviewed in the case studies to rely heavily on associations for information concerning government requirements. A typical business response to the need for information appears to involve membership in both a general business association or chamber of commerce (for information on requirements applicable to all businesses) and in an industry-specific association (for information relating to specific agencies, products, or work processes). In addition, some businesses maintained membership in an association specializing in a particular business activity, such as labor negotiations or the like.

Access to legal expertise was predominantly identified as "attorney available when needed," with most respondents needing the advice of a lawyer on government requirements between two and four times a year. It was unclear how long such sessions lasted, or with what degree of formality (and cost) they were conducted. Businesses reporting the greatest need for legal expertise relating to government requirements were in the areas of manufacturing, construction, and retail trade. The need for legal advice on government requirements also appears to increase with business size. Most businesses with zero to four employees require the services of a lawyer once or less per year, and the number of legal contacts increases fairly steadily for businesses with over five employees. There is a slight drop-off in the higher range of 100 to 249 employees, which may be a result of aberrations from a smaller sample in that range.

(With regard to legal advice, one of our initial contacts in the academic field noted that from his experience, small businesses who use an attorney *experienced* in dealing with government requirements are in the best position, but that those who use no attorney are better off than those who use inexperienced attorneys.)

Most of these points also apply to the use of accountants, the principal other source of outside expertise for small businesses.

There is an inherent frustration in seeking information on government requirements, in that no matter how much time or money is spent, there will still be information that has not yet been discovered or assimilated. The optimal goal of information expenditures would be to spend as little time and money as necessary to attain a level of sufficient information. However, such a goal relies upon a clearly defined "sufficient" level of information about government requirements, which does not seem to exist. In the absence of this clear definition, expenditures will vary according to the owner/manager's curiosity and perception of information needs.

One of the small business managers interviewed provides an example of the upper range of information expenditures. Mr. X, manager of an electronics firm, is a member of seven separate associations, subscribes to numerous research and trade publications, seeks information on government requirements from his lawyer six times a year (and from his accountant once a week), and reads between fifty and sixty reports and newsletters relating to government requirements each month. As a result of his efforts, Mr. X feels "adequately" informed about requirements applying to his business, but concludes, "There is no way you can know all the regulations that apply to you."

At the other extreme are those small businesses which from either choice or lack of resources make few if any expenditures on information. The risks of such an approach include vulnerability to disciplinary fines or other enforcement actions and the possible social costs of noncompliance. Such firms are completely reliant on agency information regarding applicable requirements. The need for a "sufficient" level of information, as defined by the agencies themselves, is especially important for these small businesses.

Use of the government agency itself as an information source appears to depend on the "relationship with government" discussed in the section entitled Psychological Costs. As a corollary, the relationship with government seems to be partly determined by the degree of clarity and consistency in the information received from the government.

Those we interviewed who frequently requested information directly from government agencies were generally quite positive about the help they had received, although certain problems were noted, especially difficulty in locating the proper agency and the appropriate person within that agency. Several people stressed the value of identifying one person in an agency who could be relied on for information and who could be held somewhat accountable.

As a final note on information costs, 28 percent of respondents to the association questionnaire (see chapter 4) identified both "money spent on professional advice" and "time spent gathering information about government requirements" as high-cost impacts on their membership.

Avoidance Costs

Forty percent of all respondents reported having challenged or appealed a government ruling or proposed regulation affecting their business. Manufacturing businesses demonstrated the greatest tendency to challenge government actions, and the percentage of respondents reporting challenges or appeals increased steadily as size of business increased. Of those who reported challenges, half had challenged government two or more times. There appeared to be an even distribution of respondents having won or lost.

Avoidance costs, or specifically, challenges to government actions, are likely to be closely related to the attitude of the small business owner/manager and to his or her "relationship with government." The seemingly high percentage of challenges among respondents to the small business questionnaire may be indicative of a bias in the sample and may be related to some of the rather strong feelings expressed in the "cumulative impacts" section of the questionnaire (see the section entitled Cumulative Impacts on Business Operations).

The case study interviews revealed a wide range of time and effort expended on gathering information and challenging government requirements. Several businesses with a history of challenges to government actions also reported especially high impacts of government requirements.

Start-Up Costs

Small businesses responding to this section reported costs similar to those for established businesses, the only differences being that new small business owners are much less familiar with most requirements affecting their businesses and the time involved tends to be proportionately higher.

Direct compliance costs prior to operation appeared to be highest in manufacturing, as might be expected.

A special problem for potential small businesses stems from delays that occur in obtaining initial licenses and permits. These delays can be extremely costly in terms of maintaining adequate financing, but the problem of delay appears to be restricted to isolated instances in a few industries (especially in innovative industries such as aquaculture). Note, however, that the *fear* of delay is widespread and reinforced by these isolated instances. Once again, those businesses which did not start because the potential owner feared delays (and we did hear of such cases in our initial interviews) are more "invisible victims" of government requirements or at least of the fear of government requirements.

A number of respondents reported difficulties in obtaining adequate information about which licenses and permits were required of them. This problem is being addressed by the ongoing efforts of Washington state's Business License Center (and similar efforts being considered by some local governments) to consolidate information and procedures in the licensing process. These efforts are based on the theory that the more consolidation of information and procedures that occurs, the more initial costs to the new small businesses will decrease.

Obviously, this section of the questionnaire did not reach those small businesses which never started because of initial confusion, delays, or the prohibitive cost of requirements. The failure of businesses to begin because of start-up costs is potentially the most profound type of impact of government requirements on small business, but no one can be sure of the extent of the problem.

Opportunity Costs

The most prevalent type of opportunity cost to small businesses involves the reluctance or inability of many small businesses to bid for government contract work because additional reporting, record keeping, and other requirements are involved. Respondents who filled out this category in our questionnaire cited lack of managerial time, costs of requirements, and uncertainty or delay as reasons for avoiding or discontinuing work under government contracts.

This type of opportunity cost appears to have the greatest impact on small businesses in the construction industries, especially in relation to equal opportunity-related reporting, record keeping, and other requirements. In some cases, the impact of these requirements may be exactly opposite of the intended impact. One medium-small electrical contractor we interviewed noted that requirements for hiring minority subcontractors on government projects had been extremely difficult to meet because many small minority subcontractors were unwilling to take on the additional administrative costs required under government contracts.

Although one can argue that costs associated with government contract work are essentially "voluntary" costs, in another sense such costs artificially limit the small business market and may have definite anticompetitive impacts.

An additional opportunity cost affecting the construction industry involves delays in government approvals for property development. One homebuilder we interviewed claimed that property development had to begin at least 2 years prior to construction to allow enough time for hearings and administrative approvals at various levels of local government. (For more information on the impact of government requirements on the homebuilding industry, see the case study interview in appendix C. Also see the works on the issue listed in the bibliography.)

Avoidance or cutbacks in product development or additional product lines or services are special problems for certain manufacturing companies. Reasons for opportunity costs in these activities included government delay of approval and lack of managerial time. One manager we interviewed pointed out that the costs and risks of product development were so high to begin with, that any additional time or money spent was enough to make product development completely infeasible. "It all boils down to where you want to spend your time—we have given up on product development."

Reasons cited for avoiding expansion into new geographic markets and change of location included uncertainty and complexity of requirements in the new location. In general, the owner/managers fear the uncertainty and complexity they predict will surround new requirements more than they fear the uncertainty and complexity they know surrounds existing requirements.

Each of the owner/managers we interviewed had at least one personal story to illustrate a particular point about government waste, inefficiency, and the like. These "horror stories" were both amusing and disturbing. In some of these cases, it was clear that, as also pointed out by several government personnel, the problems were brought on at least in part by the recalcitrance or principles of the owner/manager. In other cases, several problems involved government attitudes or inflexibility in the application of a particular rule. Some extreme examples of "horror stories" selected from appendix C are as follows:

A chemical manufacturing company was forced to drop its profit-sharing plan because of the high cost of government-required outside accounting.

A machinery manufacturer does not bid on government contracts because the owner/manager feels that it is impossible for a small business such as his to fully comply with EEO requirements.

A wholesale growing nursery was told by a representative of the Department of Agriculture that the agency would not enforce the regulation requiring the company to obtain a separate license for each chemical it uses to spray plants, but that the company would be held liable in case of a customer lawsuit or complaint.

A wholesaler of engine parts said that this year government requirements will cause him to dismiss all of his company's employees and return to a one-man shop.

In summary, opportunity costs represent one of the highest negative impacts of government requirements, but as with start-up costs (which are a type of opportunity cost), these costs are restricted to individual companies in specific industries. In many cases, the small business *perception* of requirements may have more impact than the actual cost of those requirements. Therefore, appropriate ways of addressing these problems might involve consolidation and improved access to information on government requirements, reductions in approval delays, and some recognition of special small business problems in meeting government contracting requirements.

Cumulative Impacts on Business Operations

Overview

The subsections that follow describe the range of responses to the first nine categories of cumulative impacts on company operations. Those descriptions are followed by a speculative discussion of the responses to the attitudinal questions of independence, enjoyment, and relationship with government.

Most of the questions in the cumulative impacts section were either left blank or answered with a short word or phrase such as "raises" (prices), "reduces" or "lessens" (managerial independence, enjoyment of doing business, and so on), or simply "negative" (all questions).

Price of Goods or Services

Most respondents indicated that prices had been raised by government in some way, although few were able to specify an amount (for example, "has increased prices—amount impossible to determine"). Specific causes of higher prices were identified as "taxes," "red tape," specific requirements, or higher prices charged by suppliers because of government requirements.

A number of respondents claimed that government requirements have had no effect on prices, and several noted that cost but not prices had become higher. An earlier study has demonstrated the relative inability of small businesses to pass through price increases.[1]

Of those who estimated a figure for price increase, the range of responses was between a 5 percent and a 25 percent increase, although such figures cannot be accurately substantiated by the data available.

Quality of Goods or Services

The intent of this category was interpreted in two ways, either as an implicit assumption that quality is raised or that quality is lowered. In the former case, a defensive response was "no great improvement and in some cases less quality"; in the latter case, many respondents defended the quality of their goods and services as remaining essentially unchanged. Those reporting lowered quality cited reasons such as lack of time to supervise, the need to cut corners to make up for higher government-induced costs, a decline in worker productivity, and rigid specifications which actually had served to decrease quality. A number of respondents felt that government regulations had actually improved the quality of their product.

Location of Business

In those cases where government requirements were cited as a major determinant of business location, reasons given included city taxes, zoning requirements, and antibusiness attitudes. A number of respondents expressed a desire, coupled with an inability, to move or expand, primarily as a result of zoning requirements.

A more detailed local study on factors influencing location (out-migration) was conducted recently by the Institute for Puget Sound Needs for the Seattle Department of Community Development.[2] The study ranked certain factors influencing relocation decisions among fifty-seven firms which had recently relocated (primarily manufacturing and wholesaling firms). As table 6-2 suggests, local requirements may be a relatively unimportant factor in business location decisions.

Business Growth

Reasons given for lack of growth included a drain on capital caused by high tax rates or requirements, a drain on managerial time caused by government paperwork, and a general unwillingness to grow, based on uncertainty of requirements and the desire to retain a "low profile" with respect to government regulators.

Table 6-2
Ranking and Percentage Comparison of Relocation Factors Rated Important

Ranking	% Rated Important	Factor Influencing Relocation Decisions
1	80.0	Unable to find low price in city.
2	50.9	Reduce company tax bill.
3	48.1	Avoid traffic congestion.
4	47.3	Unable to find large enough city site.
5	46.2	More or better parking.
6	40.8	Facility obsolescence due to production change.
7	38.2	Improve product distribution.
8	34.5	Moved to consolidate.
9	29.6	Avoid Seattle rules and regulations.
10	24.6	Wanted business park atmosphere.
11	20.4	Reduce executive commuting.
12	17.0	Reduce employee commuting.
13	11.1	Moved closer to major supplier.
14	3.8	Poor labor union relations.

Source: Carol A. Aaron, *Business Migration Study: An Analysis of Out Migration Patterns of Seattle Firms*, Institute for Puget Sound Needs, 1977. Reprinted with permission.

Several businesses reported business growth caused by an increase in government contract work or by other indirect government impacts. ("Positive effect: Society needs more CPAs to interpret confusing, complex, and oftentimes ridiculous forms.")

Business Profits

The category of business profits elicited a number of angry responses directed at the small business burden and at specific expenditures on requirements, especially administrative costs.

Most respondents simply wrote "reduces" or "lessens" in response to the growth and profits categories.

Competitive Position of Your Business

This category of cumulative impacts generated a variety of interesting responses. The expected response, that small companies are at a relative disadvantage vis-à-vis larger companies, was actually in the minority. Of those respondents reporting a competitive disadvantage, causes cited included perceived variations in requirements affecting competitors across national, state, and local governmental boundaries; preferential treatment given competitors by certain government programs; and a surprising animosity expressed by several "larger" small companies (and confirmed in our case study interviews) that smaller or newly established competitors are at an advantage because they are either "exempt" from certain requirements or they simply fail to comply and can thus cut costs. As one owner/manager of a larger small business told us, "We're too big to be small and too small to be big."

A large number of respondents claimed "no effect" on their competitive position; for example, "All business faces the same problems." Several reported that their competitive position had been improved by government requirements, in the sense that they have access to the "government market" because of a developed expertise in regulatory compliance.

Innovation

Many respondents reported that innovation had been reduced because of delay in approval about uncertainty of applicable requirements, time and money required to research and meet new requirements, lack of available capital, and the fear of possible government penalties.

Several respondents noted that "innovation" had increased, either through compliance with government standards or through avoidance of government requirements—"We innovate by trying to skirt government regulations."

Employment

Although one business reported hiring additional staff for government reporting, record keeping, and compliance matters, the impact of government requirements on small business employment appears to be predominantly negative. There seems to be a tendency for many businesses to intentionally keep a "low profile" (in employment size) to avoid government scrutiny. However, it is unclear how much of this concern over "visibility" is real and how much is based on the owner/manager's perception of government. Several respondents and interviewees actually reported a reduction in their workforce for this reason, and more than one owner/manager expressed an intention not to surpass the EEO cutoff limit of ninety-nine employees. In addition, the new minimum wage has caused a number of businesses to avoid hiring temporary or part-time help (especially high-school-age employees).

Reporting requirements (Washington DES, DOLI, and so on) per employee have the greatest impact on the smallest firms, where the marginal administrative costs of hiring an additional employee can be prohibitive (at least psychologically). Recruiting and related EEO requirements were also mentioned as disincentives to hiring.

In summary, and based on a limited amount of subjective data, there appear to be strong disincentives, whether real or imagined, working against an expansion of small business employment.

Relationships with Employees

Relationships with employees were generally reported as adversary, because of management enforcement of government requirements and government "encouragement" of an adversary relationship. One respondent wrote that government "tends to put a separation between employer and employee," and another wrote that government "tends to make relationships much too rigid."

However, a number of respondents said that government requirements had brought the management and employees closer together. One manager explained that a camaraderie had developed between the employees and the business, because employees identified with the problems that the business faced, especially in the area of tax reporting. He also said that specific safety and environmental requirements were often first questioned by the employees themselves.

Psychological Costs

Responses to the last three categories of the cumulative impacts section, relationship with government, managerial independence, and your enjoyment of doing business, elicited a number of strong responses which were supplemented by attached notes and letters from the respondents.

Opinions on relationship with government ranged from "As little as possible" to specific criticisms of government personnel, government forms, and aspects of the information/communication process vis-à-vis government. Most respondents who filled out this section characterized the relationship as an adversary one. Other respondents stressed a desire for a closer relationship and the necessity of maintaining a good relationship. Almost all responses in the managerial independence section indicated that independence had been reduced in restricting options, in requiring government input into management decisions, and in feelings of government "control." Enjoyment of doing business was also generally reported as being reduced, except in a few cases where respondents indicated that their enjoyment had been unaffected. On the negative side, one respondent wrote, "I enjoy playing the game with government because we win once in awhile."

Government Personnel

Small business perceptions of government personnel range from highly positive to highly negative. However, it is the negative perceptions that tend to erode the small business/government relationship and exacerbate the impacts of other aspects of compliance. Negative perceptions of government personnel involved the following types of characteristics:

Arrogance/self-righteousness/superiority

Condescension

Suspicion of business motives, distrust

Lack of understanding of business, incompetence

Lack of accountability, reluctance to make decisions, anonymity, impersonality

In particular, the combined perceptions of incompetence and condescension seem to evoke the most frustrated responses:

> Every instance in which we have been involved in providing service for a federal agency has left us with the feeling that most of their procedures and requirements are devised by people with a very meager knowledge of the subject at hand but who are firmly convinced that because they represent the government, they are "all knowing" and that everybody doing business with the government on a contract basis is basically dishonest and unintelligent.

These characteristics probably involve elements of both actual behavior and expectations or projections on the part of the small businesses. In any case, it will be important for government to address such perceptions constructively if any real improvements in the small business/government relationship are to be made.

Government Forms

Certain perceived characteristics of government forms and other written communications also tend to exacerbate negative aspects of the small business/ government relationship. Such perceptions have less to do with the actual time spent filling out the forms than with attitudes projected by the language and content of the forms. Perceived negative characteristics of government forms include:

Repetitive cross-checking questions implying lack of trust

Reports and questions for which there are no apparent reasons—purpose of questions not clear

Unexpected reports unrelated to standard business records—require extensive new research

Questions and categories that apply only to larger businesses

Impersonal bureaucratic language of forms

Authoritative or condescending language of forms

The language or rhetoric of government forms has a particularly important effect on small business perceptions of government. There is not so much a need to "simplify" the language of government forms and other written communications as there is to "humanize" the *tone* of that language.

The Commission on Federal Paperwork, in its report entitled "Information Value/Burden Assessment," generated a similar list of types of complaints about government (federal) reporting requirements. Some of these "examples of burden" are contained in the following list by category title:

Reporting too frequent

Irregular reporting periods

Filing dates not staggered

Continuous/intensive reporting in lieu of sampling

Unrealistic time frames

Unrealistic review times

Excessive audits

Excessive number of copies

Duplication of data

No standard requirements

No standard forms

Forms of the same length regardless of respondent size and capability

Irregular form sizes and other specifications

Invasions of privacy

Disclosures of confidential information

These types of complaints about government reporting forms relate more closely to the issue of administrative costs than to the small business/government relationship. However, such complaints undoubtedly also contribute to the erosion of the relationship.

Information and Communication Process

Other negative characteristics of government behavior as perceived by the small business owner/manager involve aspects of the information and communications process with government.

Some of these perceptions are similar to those voiced about government personnel. For example, one owner we interviewed, noting the superior attitude he perceived among government personnel, remarked "It's a one-way communications systems: *Down!*" Other characteristics include:

Frequent changes in requirements—unpredictability

Unreliability of telephone information

Lack of clear, concise answers—inability to get a "straight answer"

Conflicting information from different sources within an agency

Personnel who apparently have not read their agency's requirements

Interagency rivalry in a particular area

Difficulty in finding the appropriate agency

Difficulty in finding the appropriate person within an agency

Hypotheses about Psychological Costs

We directed some of our analysis specifically toward why government requirements generate more symbolic impact than their tangible costs might seem to justify. We derived several hypotheses to explain this, which together could produce the disparity between cumulative impacts and measurable ones. These hypotheses may be important in designing reform efforts because they offer targets for efforts designed to reduce the cumulative impacts.

Uncertainty

One possible cause is the uncertainty surrounding government requirements. Many firms find discovering and understanding requirements extremely difficult and will go for months or even years not knowing whether they are in compliance with all the requirements in a given area. Alternatively, they may know that they are not complying, but not know when and how government may choose to enforce the requirements. Because of the constant change in the requirements in force, businessmen may worry that they will be required to make expensive changes in their work routines or physical facilities at any time. Even when they are not required to do anything of this sort, they live with that worry.

Independence

The American romance with the idea of small business is based on the ideology that small businessmen are independent, that they call their own shots. With government in the picture, that independence is seriously threatened. The power of small businessmen to do with their businesses what they want to do, when and how they want to do it, is severely limited.

Size and Complexity

Another element of the romance with small business is that it is simpler than government or big business. The issues are fewer in number and easier to deal with.

Government agencies, which by business standards are almost always large organizations, insist on injecting complexity into the businessman's otherwise much simpler world. If government is wrestling with how to treat all races with dignity, it insists that business play a part. If government is trying to balance economic growth with environmental protection, business is dragged into that controversy as well.

The complexity is not just a substantive matter. Government agencies have complicated procedures and the power to force businessmen to follow them, even though the businessmen may have left large corporations and started small businesses precisely to avoid that sort of complexity.

Authority

Related to independence, the power to do what one wants to do, is authority, the power to make others act and to avoid doing what others want you to do. For some businessmen, a small business offers a chance to be "the boss" and to have no boss themselves. Even if a small businessman cannot do everything he wants to do, there is no one overseeing him. Here again, government diminishes that feeling, by telling people what to do.

Interest

The final hypothesis on this list is that small businessmen are simply not interested in many of the things they are required to do. A small business hopes that not only will the problems it faces be few in number, but also they will be ones the owner/manager can choose. In one case study, a respondent reported that although he could not say that filling out a particular form took an excessively long time, the person doing it found the task so excrutiatingly boring that it seemed to take forever. If an owner/manager is involved in small business to avoid the bureaucratic structure of larger companies, government requirements may represent an unwelcome sense of bureaucracy in his activities.

Relation to Reform

These hypotheses are not explanations; nonetheless, they are consistent with suggestions others have offered as explanations and they could help guide reform efforts. For instance, for those who resent governmental authority, government agencies and their personnel are apt to seem high-handed and arbitrary in their enforcement of regulations. For those who prize independence, the government seems meddling. For those who lack interest, the government seems too anxious to involve small businessmen in its concerns.

Possible reforms based on these ideas include (1) training in ways to minimize sources of conflict for government personnel who interact with business; (2) more explanation for small businesses who want to know why the government is involved in their activities; and (3) simplification of required tasks for those who prefer to be bothered as little as possible.

A Method for Estimating Standard Annual Costs

Table 6-3 presents a method for estimating the annual cost of government requirements to an individual small business, based on the cost categories defined in the small business questionnaire. A cost figure generated by this method would be a rough estimate of short-term measurable costs. It would not include opportunity costs, psychological impacts, or other long-term cumulative impacts. Obviously, these latter costs are "quantifiable" in some fashion, but they are not "measurable" in the sense of hours worked or dollars spent. If data from the small business questionnaire are used with this method, the cost figures generated are of course subject to the same qualifications as the data themselves. In particular, using the average cost figures from the questionnaire data and then multiplying the result by the number of firms in Washington state will not necessarily yield the total cost for the state, because those responding to the questionnaire are not necessarily representative of all firms. However, using the extremes of the questionnaire data should yield the range in costs for individual small businesses, since the questionnaire respondents are likely to include the extreme (for reasons discussed at the beginning of chapter 3).

The method presented in table 6-3 also requires the use of other data, such as the owner/manager's annual salary. In the results presented here, we have tried to use reasonable figures and present ranges. Others can recalculate using different figures if they prefer.

The method presented includes standard or expected costs, unexpected costs, and voluntary costs. *Standard or expected costs* include license, permit, and registration fees, administrative costs, and basic information costs. In other words, they include costs incurred by all businesses to some extent every year. *Unexpected costs* include direct compliance costs such as changes in work routines, changes in physical facilities, and disciplinary fines. Unexpected administrative costs (such as a reporting form that comes as a surprise to the owner) are not included in this category, but in the preceding one. We feel use of the term *unexpected* is not appropriate where a small business is aware of its noncompliance with a particular requirement. *Voluntary costs* include only the costs of challenges to government actions. Voluntary administrative costs, such as the additional reporting and record keeping required under government contracts, are not included in this category, but rather in the first one.

Table 6-3
Method for Estimating Annual Costs of Government Requirements to an Individual Small Business

Direct Compliance Costs:

License/permit fees (standard) $_____
Registration fees $_____
Filings fees $_____

Total $_____

Changes in work routines (unexpected)

Administrative time × rate $_____
Loss of revenue $_____
Retraining costs $_____

Total $_____ $_____
                                                                  (Amortize)

Changes in physical facilities (unexpected)

Cost of managerial time spent to supervise
    and implement change $_____
Cost of employee time spent to implement
    change $_____
Cost of outside consultant or contractor $_____
Purchase price of new equipment or
    materials $_____
Increase in operating costs resulting
    from change $_____
Other costs $_____

Total $_____ $_____
                                                                  (Amortize)

Disciplinary fines (unexpected) $_____ $_____
                                                                  (Amortize)

Administrative Costs (Standard):

Inspections: Hourly cost of person
    Hours per year _____ × guiding   _____   = $_____

Percent of owner/
    manager's time _____ × yearly salary _____   = $_____

Reporting and applications:

Hours per year   _____
    plus
record keeping
Hours per year   _____
    minus
owner/manager's time (20
hours per each 1% listed
above)   _____
    equals

                              Hourly cost of person
                              primarily responsible
Total   _____ ×   (bookkeeper) _____   = $_____

Miscellaneous administrative costs   = $_____

Table 6-3 continued

Administrative Costs (Alternative Method):

		Total administrative costs (based on a percentage of annual revenue		
Percent of administrative costs	_____ X	by firm size and industry) _____	=	$_____

Information and Avoidance Costs

Annual cost of subscription services (standard) $_____

Annual cost of association memberships (standard) $_____

Annual cost of managerial time in research on government
    requirements (standard) $_____

Annual cost of employee time in research on government
    requirements (standard) $_____

Annual cost of legal information on requirements (standard) $_____

Annual cost of accountants or other outside specialists for
    information on requirements (standard/voluntary) $_____

Challenges (voluntary)

Contributions	$_____
Cost of managerial time	$_____
Cost of employee time	$_____
Legal fees, etc.	$_____
Total	$_____

                                                                         $_____
                                                                        (Amortize)

Special costs not included above $_____

*Approximate annual short-term cost of government requirements
to individual business* $_____

Standard or expected costs occur regularly, so they can be estimated on an annual basis. Unexpected and voluntary costs, in contrast, do not occur regularly (although they may occur more than once) and so can be either added to the estimate for the year in which they occur or spread across the estimates for a number of years (amortized, in some sense). In our estimates, we have amortized such costs over a 5-year period and added them to "standard or expected costs" to estimate the annual cost of government requirements for various categories of individual businesses.

In this example, we made several assumptions, largely on the low side. First, we estimated the hourly rates for an owner/manager and a bookkeeper to be $10 and $5, respectively. Second, we estimated standard information costs at $50 for subscriptions (although commercial subscription services usually start from $200); $50 for 1 hour per year of legal advice; and $100 for a single association membership (although many businesses in our sample reported membership in several associations). One reason for these conservative estimates on information costs is that subscriptions and association memberships are

only partially attributable to the need for information on government requirements. Also, there is an extreme range in expenditures on information, and
many of these costs may be termed "voluntary."

The key variable determining the total amount of standard annual cost is
the time spent by the owner/manager on reporting, record keeping, and inspections. The impact of this variable will vary by industry, by size of business,
and by assumed salary rates for the owner/manager. In the preceding example,
total annual cost will vary considerably with different assumptions about the
owner/manager's pay. For instance, assuming 2,000 working hours per year:

At $10 per hour, total annual cost = $1,608

At $20 per hour, total annual cost = $2,271

At $30 per hour, total annual cost = $2,934

At $40 per hour, total annual cost = $3,597

Using the $10 per hour assumption, annual median cost of time spent by
the owner/manager on reporting and record keeping alone varies by industry
and by size of firm (using the data already shown in figures 6-12 and 6-14)
from $160 per year in finance to $1,000 per year in construction, and from
$400 per year in the largest firms (100 to 249 employees) to $920 per year
in the next largest firms (50 to 99 employees).

As shown in table 6-4, the total of administrative costs and license fees
varies from $3,080 per year in construction to $905 per year in services, and
from $660 per year for the smallest firms (0 to 4 employees) to $8,660 per
year for the largest (100 to 249 employees). Note how the administrative
costs are disproportionately high for smaller firms. Even with the assumption
that the biggest firm in each size category had only the median expenses (it
almost certainly had more than the median), costs per employee ranged from
$165 in the 4-employee firm to $35 in the 249-employee firm.

Table 6-5 shows the cost figures from four actual cases. These examples
are most notable for the wide range of costs they involve. The table shows the
range of costs per employee and as a percent of revenue. Of course, not all costs
are directly related to the number of employees, but costs that are related may
be a crucial factor in a decision about whether or not to hire the next employee.

Digest of Costs by Category

This section presents a digest of the costs discussed in detail in the eight preceding sections. The digest is *not* a summary in the sense of briefly covering *all*
the points raised previously; instead it briefly covers the *important* points.

Table 6-4
Annual Cost of License Fees and Standard Administrative Costs, by Industrial Division and Size of Firm

Cost Category	Industrial Division					
	Construction	Manufacturing	Wholesale	Retail	Finance	Service
Licenses	$ 708	$ 170	$ 300	$ 190	$ 282	$ 100
Inspections	100	160	50	38	2	500
Reports and record keeping						
Owner/manager's time	1,000	600	400	700	160	500
Others' time	950	580	585	315	445	20
Miscellaneous (copying, etc.)	322	600	410	250	325	10
Totals	$3,080	$2,110	$1,745	$1,493	$1,214	$ 90

Cost Category	Size of Firm (Number of Employees)					
	0-4	5-9	10-19	20-49	50-99	100-2
Licenses	$ 147	$ 125	$ 300	$ 250	$ 200	$ 49
Inspections	3	8	35	99	240	11
Reports and record keeping						
Owner/manager's time	460	500	900	800	920	40
Others' time	–	550	380	1,100	795	5,98
Miscellaneous (copying, etc.)	50	235	200	567	1,010	1,68
Total	$ 660	$1,418	$1,815	$2,816	$3,165	$8,66
Per Employee[a]	$ 165	$ 157	$ 95	$ 57	$ 32	$ 3

[a]This figure is very conservative, in that it assumes that all firms in a particular size category are the upper limit of that category and that all of them had the median amount of expenses.

Table 6-5
Estimated Annual Measurable Costs of Government Requirements from Selected Actual Costs[a]

Type of Firm	No. of Employees	Annual Revenue	Annual Measurable Costs	Cost per Employee	Cost per Revenue$
Electrical contractor	3	24,000	4,267	1,422	18%
Chemical manufacturer	33	2,300,000	3,805	115	–
General contractor	35	5,000,000	38,385	1,097	1%
Equipment manufacturer	60	2,500,000	9,805	163	–

[a]The cases were shown as illustrations of the *range* of costs, not because they were typical. The primary criteron in choosing these four was the completeness with which they had filled out the questionnaire.

Direct Compliance Costs

The annual cost of *license, permit, and registration fees* ranged from 0 to over $10,000, with a median response of approximately $200 per year. Businesses in construction, wholesale, and finance reported the highest costs in this category.

Twenty-two percent of respondents reported *changes in work routines* to comply with government requirements, with the highest percentage of responses falling in the construction (34 percent) and finance (22 percent) industries. Types of changes reported included retraining employees, changes in hiring procedures, new approaches to employee relations, changes in accounting procedures, and so on.

Thirty-two percent of respondents reported required *changes to physical facilities*, with 16 percent reporting two or more required changes. A high percentage of manufacturers reported changes to physical facilities (64 percent), with cost estimates ranging up to several hundred thousand dollars. The median cost to those who made physical changes was approximately $6,000.

Fifteen percent of respondents reported having to pay *civil or criminal fines* for alleged violations of government requirements, with most of the impact felt in the manufacturing and construction industries (31 and 20 percent of respondents, respectively). Of those businesses reporting fines, about one-third listed two or more fines since 1970.

Out data indicate that the incidences of required changes in work routines, changes to physical facilities, and disciplinary fines all tend to increase with business size. Reports of equal employment opportunity-related impacts also increased with firm size. This observation tends to support a conclusion made in an earlier study that a kind of "tail-off" effect exists in government enforcement, in that smaller firms are often overlooked in enforcement of required changes to physical facilities.[3]

Required changes to physical facilities are the most significant type of direct compliance costs. Although changes to physical facilities do not represent a standard or expected cost for most small businesses, the costs can be severe when it does occur. The combined costs of new equipment, installation, and managerial and employee time spent in implementing the change can directly reduce small business profits, either because of a loss in revenue caused by a markup in product price or, more likely, because of the small firm's inability to pass through cost increases.[4] If the costs of a physical change are particularly high, they can also put a strain on the small firm's already limited available capital and thus act as a serious constraint to the small firm's growth.

Administrative Costs

The median annual time reported spent on *government inspections* was 4.3 hours for all respondents, ranging up to medians of 10 hours per year in construction and 16 hours per year in manufacturing. The median amount of time spent on government inspection appears to increase with business size. In some larger businesses (especially manufacturing), inspections were handled by a foreman or plant manager. In most smaller companies, the owner/manager was primarily responsible for guiding inspectors.

The median number of hours per year spent on *government reporting* was 72 hours in our sample. Firms in construction (140 hours) and manufacturing (120 hours) reported higher medians, and firms in services (39 hours) and retail trade (33 hours) reported lower ones. Time spent on government reporting increased steadily with business size.

The distribution of hours per year spent on government *record keeping* is parallel to the distribution for reporting, except that the relative positions of construction and manufacturing are reversed, and the median figure for retail businesses is relatively much higher (possibly due to inclusion of sales tax records). In all industries, the median response for the time spent on government record keeping (100 hours per year) was higher than the median figure for government reporting (72 hours per year). Median figures for manufacturing (156 hours per year) and for construction (150 hours per year) were significantly higher than the overall figure.

As with reporting and record keeping, the level of miscellaneous administrative costs (travel, duplicating, and so on) appears to increase steadily with business size.

The amount of time spent directly by the owner/manager on government-related administrative tasks is primarily dependent on business size. Small businesses in the construction industry reported the highest percentages of time spent by the owner/manager on reporting and record keeping.

Information Costs

A majority of firms in our sample did not feel adequately informed about the nature and extent of government requirements which affect them, yet we noted a reluctance on the part of some businesses to spend more than a minimum amount of time or money on gathering information. Several people suggested that some government agencies may provide *enough* information, but in forms too overwhelming or complex to guide the small business. Coupled with this apparent reluctance to gather information are fears of possible enforcement actions by government for noncompliance and frustration at receiving inadequate information. However, some of the firms in our sample appeared to spend much larger amounts of time and money on regulatory information than did others. The use of lawyers and accountants for information on government requirements appeared to increase by business size.

There is an inherent frustration in seeking information on government requirements, in that no matter how much time or money is spent, there will still be information not yet discovered or assimilated. The optimal goal of information expenditures would be to spend as little time and money as necessary to attain a sufficient level of information. However, such a goal relies on a clearly defined "sufficient" level of information about government requirements, which does not seem to exist. In the absence of a clear definition of sufficient information, expenditures will vary according to the owner/manager's curiosity and perception of information needs.

Finally, most small businesses are highly dependent on their associations for information about government requirements. This is especially true of those businesses which spend no more on government information than their annual association membership fees.

Avoidance Costs

Forty percent of all respondents reported having challenged or appealed a government ruling of proposed regulation affecting their businesses. Manufacturing businesses demonstrated the greatest tendency to challenge government actions. The percentage of respondents reporting challenges or appeals increased with business size. Of those who reported challenges, half had challenged government two or more times. There appeared to be an even distribution of respondents having won or lost such appeals.

Start-Up Costs

Start-up costs involve initial compliance, administrative, and information costs incurred when a business is first established. Costly delays or prohibitive barriers to entry appear to exist only in specific industries (such as aquaculture). For most businesses, start-up costs are similar to costs incurred by existing businesses, except that information costs tend to be higher, since the owner/manager may not yet be familiar with applicable government requirements.

Opportunity Costs

The most prevalent types of opportunity costs related to government requirements include reluctance to hire additional employees because of increased "visibility" or possible increases in administrative costs and reluctance or inability to bid for government contract work based on perceptions of prohibitively expensive administrative and direct compliance costs.

Cumulative Impacts on Business Operations

Although this study has focused primarily on short-term costs of government requirements, a majority of respondents to questions on cumulative impacts reported definite negative impacts of government requirements on their long-term business operations. They remained the same size or grew smaller (in employment or sales) instead of growing or grew slower than they might have otherwise. Although few respondents were able to estimate long-term impacts with any degree of precision, the fact that these impacts cannot be quantified easily is not particularly important. The perception that there will be negative impacts is quite significant because it underlies plans for growth and business development.

Psychological Costs

The drain on an owner/manager's energy and motivation can be even more important than any amount of time or money spent on government requirements. This "psychological cost" of government requirements is closely related to the owner/manager's relationship with government, as influenced by perceived characteristics of government forms, personnel, and information, as well as by the attitudes of the owner/manager. According to one informed observer, "the key words are *bitterness* and *frustration.* "

The disparity between psychological and tangible costs may involve several simultaneous reactions on the part of the owner/manager: tensions caused by uncertainty over requirements, perceived constraints to personal independence by an outside authority, and the tedious nature of many government administrative requirements, which may lead the owner/manager to feel that the entrepreneurial role is being bureaucratized or stifled.

Estimate of Total Short-Term Costs

Using the method outlined earlier, one can estimate the median cost of all "short-term costs" (including direct compliance, administrative, information, and avoidance costs and not including opportunity costs, start-up costs, long-term impacts on business operations, or psychological costs). Note that the information-cost estimate and hourly figures used are very low in order to keep the estimate conservative.

Table 6-6 estimates standard or expected annual costs by assuming a hypothetical company reporting precisely the same costs as the median response from the small business questionnaire.

Table 6-6
Estimate of Median Short-Term Costs

Standard Direct Costs				
License/registration/filing fees	Median	=	$	200
Standard Administrative Costs				
Inspections—Hours per year (median = 4.3) × hourly rate of owner/manager ($10)		=	$	43
Reporting and record keeping—percent of owner/ manager's time (median = 3.1%) × yearly salary ($20,000)		=	$	620
Reporting and applications—Hours per year (median = 72)				
plus				
Record keeping—Hours per year (median = 100)				
minus				
Owner/manager's time reported above (3.1% of 2,000 hours = 63 hours)				
equals				
Total (109 hours) × hourly rate of bookkeeper ($5)		=	$	545
Standard Information Costs				
Subscription services		=	$	50
Legal advice (1 hour per year at $50/hr)		=	$	50
Association memberships (1)		=	$	100
Standard Short-term Costs		=	$	1,608

Note: See the section entitled A Method for Estimating Standard Annual Costs for a more detailed discussion of this table.

Notes

1. Charleswater Associates, Inc., *The Impact on Small Business Concerns of Government Regulations that Force Technological Change.* Final report, prepared for U.S. Small Business Administration, Washington, D.C., September 1975.

2. Carol A. Aaron, *Business Migration Study: An Analysis of Out-Migration Patterns of Seattle Firms*, Institute for Puget Sound Needs, 1977.

3. Charleswater Associates, Inc., *The Impact on Small Business Concerns.*

4. Ibid.

7

Findings of Fact: Part 3

Analysis of Other Points of View

Most of chapters 5 and 6 are based on data provided by small businesses themselves. This chapter reports the results of our attempts to include other points of view concerning the problems of costs imposed by government requirements. The first section discusses points of view from government agencies, using the results of some of our initial interviews and our mail survey of local, state, and federal agencies. The second section discusses points of view from associations of businesses, using the results of other initial interviews and our mail survey of association executives. The third section discusses the important points raised by the PSI members and others who advised us in reviewing the first draft of our findings. This chapter concludes with an identification of some existing programs or agencies involved in efforts to reduce the costs of government requirements.

Points of View of Government Agencies

Responses to the government questionnaire, along with initial interviews (and repeated follow-up visits), have convinced us that government agency personnel are concerned about their relationship with small businesses under their jurisdiction. In addition, a number of agencies have mechanisms in place both to improve input from small businesses and to account for their special problems in implementation.

In general, federal and state government agencies are likely to give special consideration to the costs to small businesses of *proposed* requirements or procedures, while only federal agencies tend to have rules by which smaller companies are either exempted from or given special consideration in *implementation* of requirements.

Among questionnaire respondents, evaluations of the information exchange and communications process and the relationship between small business and government were highly positive, with few exceptions. A large majority of federal, state, and local agency respondents felt that many small businesses under their jurisdiction have *adequate* information on the agency's requirements, and almost all respondents characterized their agency's relationship with small business as positive in some way. However, as pointed out earlier, the *amount* of information could be adequate, while the *form* of the information is not.

This overwhelmingly positive response obviously conflicts with the attitudes expressed by respondents to the small business questionnaire. It may simply be that many government personnel were reluctant to express their views on the subject candidly in a standardized questionnaire from a study funded wholly by private sources. (One government respondent wrote "Unfair question! How am I supposed to answer?" when asked to characterize his agency's relationship with Washington state small businesses.) However, if these responses represent actual perceptions on the part of most agency personnel, either there is a real lack of communication between small business and government (or our small business sample is biased in totally unexpected ways).

We did receive some very candid comments from government personnel over the phone and in person, which tended to contradict the overwhelmingly positive responses in the questionnaire. These comments, involving the attitude of some small businesses toward government, were more expressions of concern than explicit criticisms. One government official defended government inspectors, pointing out that the nature of "enforcement" is bound to create antagonism, and that small businessmen generally have the attitude that "you're here to put me out of business." The hostility thus expressed and the defensive reactions on the part of the inspectors tend to create a set of self-fulfilling expectations on both sides. This same local official noted that inspectors "have to write fines" and are generally sympathetic to the businessman's problems. (It should be mentioned that the small business owner/managers we spoke to were far less critical of field inspectors than of more anonymous impersonal "bureaucrats" with whom they had never had personal contact.) A third point with regard to inspections was made by another government employee who expressed frustration that many businessmen simply do not listen to inspectors who advise them to make changes and are thus cited for repeat violations.

An observation made by another government official should serve as an appropriate conclusion to this brief discussion of the government perspective. This official told us that it is the small business owner/manager who resists and appeals government requirements "on principle," objecting to government intervention in general, who ends up with the highest costs and spends huge amounts of money and time fighting requirements, wasting resources far out of proportion with the minimal costs involved in compliance. We were told that these same businesses often have simultaneous problems with many agencies at once and often exhibit the most unhealthy labor/management relationships.

In summary, the government personnel we contacted were concerned about their relationship with small business and characterized information and relations as positive, but they implied in some of the interviews and phone discussions that the attitude of the owner/manager may be as much a determinant of total costs as the actions of government agencies.

Points of View of Association Executives

The following discussion is an analysis of selected portions of the questionnaire. In response to the question "Do you feel that your members are adequately informed about government requirements which affect their business?" a majority of chambers of commerce responded "no." Association responses were evenly divided between "yes" and "no." We then asked respondents to rate the following six general options "to improve the level and quality of information on government requirements available to small business":

Through an expanded role for individual associations?

Through increased coordination of government-related activities among different associations?

Through a state-run information office?

Through a new federal department or federal "information locator" system?

Through a central private-sector clearinghouse for associations and individual businesses?

Through a series of training sessions for association staff members?

The most popular of these options were an expanded role for individual associations, increased coordination among associations, and establishment of a private-sector clearinghouse. The option of a new federal or state department received little support, and even drew a number of unsolicited negative responses ("Let's keep government out of it—we don't need to add another layer of bureaucracy.")

Several respondents gave their own ideas for improving information on government requirements. Some of the more interesting comments follow.

Publish a single index of rules and regulations with brief abstracts and sources for further information, possibly by industry.

Use more prominent subject identification on agency proposals and so on. Eliminate use of legal-length paper.

Publish a *Washington State Register*, similar to the *Federal Register*.

Establish an industry clearinghouse or association subscriber service.

Establish a member subscriber service; that is, employ several attorneys or law researchers to maintain current files of regulations affecting a particular industry.

Improve the ability of small businesses to monitor what the agencies are doing or proposing; identify specialists and experts in specific areas who can be called on for assistance.

Write agency publications and regulations in laymen's terms instead of legal jargon; verify that the information is correct before sending it out (sometimes statutes have been amended and the amendments have not been included in the published version).

Include firms on all relevant agency mailing lists. "Too often agencies don't know we exist."

Table 7-1 shows the types of government compliance costs the association executives considered to be high for their memberships. This ranking of compliance costs closely corresponds to the results of our mail survey of small businesses; it is also valuable in providing a "weighting" of information and opportunity costs in relation to more tangible types of impacts.

A recurrent theme in our initial interviews and among responses to the trade association questionnaire was the lack of small business participation in the political process. One association executive's comment is indicative of this perception:

Small businessmen should become more active and alert about proposed legislation that affects their business and should let their representatives and senators know how they feel. I feel protests from several small businessmen carry more weight than protests from the large companies.

Table 7-1
Types of Compliance Costs Reported as High by Association Executives

% of Respondents Reporting High Cost to Their Membership	Types of Compliance Costs
65	Time spent on record keeping for government purposes.
50	Time spent filling out government forms.
40	Direct compliance costs (to change physical facilities, work routines, staff, etc.)
28	Money spent on professional advice (lawyers, accountants, etc.).
23	Opportunities foregone due to cost or complexity of government requirements.
20	License/permit/registration fees.
19	Time and money spent challenging or appealing government requirements.
14	Time spent on inspections.
–	Disciplinary fines.

Respondents to our small business survey may be more "activist" than those in the general small business population (especially in light of the fact that 40 percent reported some type of challenge to government actions). However, based on the comments of association executives and our initial contacts, it appears that lack of political participation is in fact characteristic of the small business population as a whole.

One small business owner we interviewed provided an example of the highly "activist" small business. In addition to being active in local politics, this small business owner has taken several trips to Washington, D.C. at his own expense to testify on proposed legislation or to negotiate with agency personnel directly. An active member of several associations, as well as an elected official in local government, he also noted a general lack of small business political involvement: "One of the biggest shames in this country is the tendency of a lot of small businessmen not to be involved in politics. . . . It's foolhardy to say I'm too involved in the business to worry about politics."

Advisor Review

We first presented our findings in a draft report that was reviewed by PSI members and others (including academics and activists) who acted as our advisors. They raised several major points which we have tried to incorporate in this final version of the report.

A number of suggestions related to presentation. These are reflected in the format of this book. The advice we received was to present research results in traditional form (for example, explain objectives and methodology in some detail, separate findings of fact from policy implications, and the like) and then address the special needs of busy activists by including an executive summary, concluding sections at various points in the text, and the like.

A second set of suggestions related to our use of case studies plus mail surveys in order to gather data. In general, our advisors thought that this approach was appropriate for gathering largely tangible data for exploratory purposes, but they cautioned us against generalizing too much from this sample.

A third set of suggestions related to the interpretation of the data. Here the question was not what the costs are, but whether the costs we have identified are heavy or light. A finding that median tangible short-term costs (*not* including any taxes) for small businesses can be estimated as approximately $1,600 per year does not, in itself, say whether costs are acceptable or too high. A finding that 25 percent of our sample has been involved in disciplinary proceedings may represent an active use of one of the only dispute-resolution mechanisms available to small business, or it may indicate a strong alienation between business and government. We need to compare these results with information and value judgments outside the scope of our data-gathering in order to interpret these findings.

We agreed with almost all the points raised by our advisors and made a special effort to incorporate their suggestions in the final draft.

Organizations Involved in Reducing the Costs Imposed by Government Requirements

A listing of national organizations involved in small business and regulatory reform, based on our initial interviews, follows.

Congress

House Small Business Committee, subcommittee on special small business problems

Senate Select Committee on Small Business

Executive

U.S. Small Business Administration
Office of Advocacy
Office of Energy, Environment, and Competitive Structure
Office of Planning, Research, and Data Management

General Accounting Office, Division of Regulatory Analysis

Office of Management and Budget
Regulatory Policy and Reports Management Division—Federal Paperwork Commission, Implementation
Data Coordination Branch—Impact Value/Burden Assessment Task Force

Federal Trade Commission, Bureau of Economics

Council on Wage and Price Stability

Department of the Treasury, Small Business Advisory Committee

White House Conference on Small Business—Upcoming

Private Sector

Business Advisory Council on Federal Reports

Citizens' Commission on Paperwork Reduction

National Small Business Association

National Federation of Independent Business

Small Business Legislative Council—includes NSBA and other associations

U.S. Chamber of Commerce, Citizens' Choice

Business Roundtable; Arthur Anderson Company conducting study on cost of requirements to larger business

American Enterprise Institute for Public Policy Research

Outside Washington, D.C. Area

Center for the Study of American Business, Washington University, St. Louis, Missouri

Harvard faculty project in regulatory reform, Harvard University, Cambridge, Massachusetts

8 Policy Implications

Introduction

As stated in chapter 3, an important purpose of this study was to provide central direction and impetus for an active subsequent effort to reduce the costs and impacts of government requirements on small business. This chapter spells out our view of the policy implications of this study in order to provide this initial direction. It is divided into three sections. The first section discusses guidelines that we think should apply to any and all reform efforts. The next section discusses the implications that stem from each category of cost we have identified and analyzed. The last section presents a list of suggestions (they are not "alternatives" because they could be implemented in combination with each other) we think meet the necessary general guidelines.

Here again, we think these implications are relevant outside of Washington state as well. Washington is not that different from other states, and neither the problems nor their solutions are likely to vary in broad outline from state to state. At the same time, we realize that subtle but important differences among states will probably lead to differences in both the priorities and specific details of potentially effective reform efforts.

Guidelines for Initiating and Designing Reform Efforts

In the course of our study, we identified a number of important criteria to be considered in planning for an active, multifaceted effort to reduce the costs of government requirements to small business. Perhaps the most important of these points is the need for a constructive, conciliatory approach to reform, as opposed to the adversary approach that often characterizes both sides of the business/government relationship.

In making this point, it should be emphasized that we are not being critical of either government or business. Further, no useful purpose is served by attempting to establish right or wrong or by assigning blame for how the antagonism developed. Our concern is with acknowledging reality as it exists today and highlighting the importance of dealing constructively with the issue as a first step in reform. Pragmatically, reform in this problem area cannot be brought about by either the private sector or the public sector working alone.

Any effort to reduce the costs of government requirements on small business must recognize the possible tradeoffs between reducing specific costs and alleviating general antagonisms. If the responses to the small business questionnaire are at all representative of the general small business population in Washington state, programs aimed at specific agencies or requirements may not be nearly as important as efforts to reform the business/government relationship, especially through aspects of the communications/information process. Even if the strong feelings expressed in the cumulative impacts section are entirely a result of a biased sample, it is clearly these respondents who are most in need of a positive program to alleviate the burdens, whether real or imagined, of an adversary relationship with government.

Thus potential reform efforts should seek the joint participation of government representatives, association executives, labor leaders, and small business owner/managers. This type of joint effort is not only needed to improve the business/government relationship, but it also may be instrumental in gaining the public-sector support necessary to achieve significant reforms. A joint business/government effort might also serve to legitimize the activities of what might otherwise be perceived as yet another "business lobby."

The first major task confronting any reform effort will be to determine where in the regulatory process to intervene: Should reform address requirements or implementation? Legislation or agency rulemaking? Proposed or existing requirements? The public-sector action or the private-sector response? What level of government should be the focus of reform?

This book has focused on the costs, as opposed to the benefits, of government requirements, with the idea that potential reductions in cost can be achieved without altering the intent of a given requirement. To the extent that reform efforts follow the lead of this book, a similar approach may be called for in selecting reform efforts. The type of broad-based reform effort suggested by this book should focus more on administrative procedures and the general regulatory process than on the issue of whether a particular set of requirements is "worthwhile." Such a value-free approach to reform is important in enlisting the support of the public sector. The approach is also important in reducing costs to small business without inadvertently recreating the "social costs" that a requirement was originally intended to alleviate.

To achieve *social goals* with a minimum of *business cost* will require a creative effort by everyone, and such an effort will probably not take place unless business and government work together on the problem. A broad-based reform effort should avoid overly specific issues. While there may be specific requirements that are especially costly and of questionable value, these can be dealt with through individual associations and the existing political process. In the course of our research, numerous examples of such requirements were described to us, and in most cases both the business people and their associations were aware of the specific problem and were working to correct it. In this sense, a reform program acting under the same broad mandate as this study should be careful not to become involved in specific controversies in specific industries, but rather seek solutions to the more comprehensive problems faced by small businesses in general.

Similarly, broad-based reform efforts should address the general problems of "small business" as opposed to specific problems of individual firms. Regulatory problem solving and advice for individual firms is best left to the lawyers, accountants, and associations that are already performing this function (in some cases, reform efforts might work toward improving the quality of these services without becoming directly involved in their delivery). Similarly, financial problems of individual businesses should be left to those businesses and their existing advisors, while reform programs might work toward improving the climate for and availability of financing for small business generally.

Reform efforts should use existing organizations wherever possible to reduce any duplication of effort and to improve efficiency and cooperation among the plethora of public and private organizations within the state. An existing organization or coalition of existing organizations should be as well equipped to handle implementation of reform as a new private or governmental body. For example, individual associations are often the best experts on specific regulatory problems affecting their industry, and they should be used to the greatest extent possible. Likewise, existing governmental organizations, such as the U.S. Small Business Administration or Washington state's Business License Center or Small Business Office, can often adapt to be just as effective in performing a new function as an entirely new agency.

A final general criterion in designing a reform program is the advantage of focusing reform efforts at the state government level. Although many of the heaviest impacts, both psychological and in terms of direct cost, occur on the federal level, requirements may be growing fastest at the state level. In addition, the state is small enough to provide an opportunity to involve a high percentage of the leadership of both government and business in joint reform efforts. The state focus could provide the most fruitful return on reform efforts. The state is an appropriate testing ground for innovative programs (such as the Business License Center) which may evolve into national examples of successful regulatory reform. If consolidation is a major emphasis of a reform program, the state is a manageable area in which to attempt a trial consolidation of federal, state, and local forms and administrative procedures.

Detailed Implications of the Study's Findings for Reform Efforts

Of course, the major value of these data to the project is the ability they give us and others to evaluate current ideas for reform in the light of detailed information about how requirements actually affect small businesses. As mentioned in chapter 1, the rhetoric about this subject has far exceeded the research.

We have divided this section into two parts: (1) a discussion of each kind of cost and the reforms people have suggested for reducing that cost, and (2) a ranking of these efforts in terms of the seriousness of the problem they are trying to solve.

Direct Compliance Costs

Understanding direct compliance costs is difficult for two reasons. First, major instances of these costs crop up in individual firms in particular industries regarding specific requirements. Very few general reforms seem appropriate for dealing with widely different specific situations. At the same time, taking on each situation one after another does not seem feasible because the number of situations is large and new ones arise all the time.

The second reason these costs are difficult to analyze stems from the fact that many businesses are likely to be unintentionally out of compliance because they are unaware of a particular requirement that applies to them. With a limited enforcement budget, the relevant agency may not know of the noncompliance. As a consequence, these costs have somewhat limited impact now, but if a situation arose in which the firm had to make a decision about compliance, it would be faced with either the costs of changing work routines or physical facilities or the costs that stem from challenging the application of the requirement. In this case, designing reform is difficult because the impacts are only potential.

The pressure for reform stems both from the idea that these impacts could be widespread, even if they are not now, and from the dramatic nature of some of the specific impacts that do occur. The reforms that are suggested generally involve having better representation for the businessman in the decision-making process surrounding the imposition of a requirement and its eventual application. For instance, one set of reforms would either encourage or require agencies to perform an assessment of their proposed requirements on small businesses and would either encourage or require the agencies to get the businessmen involved in the decision making. One promising idea that emerged from our interviews involves assembling a group of small businessmen to act as advisors or "watchdogs" over both rulemaking and rule applications. In some circumstances, such an operation seems not only to reduce the direct impacts, but also to aid the general relationship between business and government.

Another set of reforms is designed to provide firms better information about which requirements apply to them and how they might most effectively comply. Several agencies have experimented with "employer consultants" who visit firms with advice instead of citations. By and large, these efforts have been disappointing. The consultants have found establishing the requisite trust in their good faith and expertise extremely difficult. Our research suggests that perhaps trade associations or other private associations could perform this role, since theoretically people from the industry would be more effective in establishing the necessary trust.

A final set of reforms would eliminate or adjust the application of particular requirements to small businesses, the so-called two-tier approach. The idea has much merit in theory. We have already discussed how smaller firms might be better able to change work routines, while larger firms might be better able to change physical facilities. Consequently, a regulation that required large firms to change physical facilities and small firms to change work routines should have less total impact than one that required both to do the same thing. The trouble with this theory in practice is that it faces the same problem mentioned at the beginning of this section: to be effective, the tiers have to be set for specific requirements facing specific firms in specific industries. Designing a general approach would be extremely difficult.

In summary, our analysis suggests that achieving reductions in direct compliance will probably require the active involvement of small businessmen and their private associations. Unlike some other costs, compliance costs probably cannot be efficiently reduced by sweeping general actions.

Administrative Costs

All our sources of data confirm that the main priority in this category is not to reduce the time requirements generally so much as it is to reduce the drain on the owner/manager's time. In a few cases, the distinction may be quite important, for a complicated form that only the owner/manager can fill out may have a far greater impact on the business than simple forms that bookkeepers can fill out. In other cases, the distinction between the owner/manager's time and others' time will be less significant, for anything that makes the forms easier to fill out also increases the ability of the owner/manager to delegate the task to someone else.

Several reform options address the question of simplifying the government reporting and record-keeping requirements. One suggestion is that the various government agencies distribute instructions with each form, so that the owner/ manager can hand the instructions and the form to a subordinate. The second suggestion is that the government agencies publish "outlines" for providing immediate answers to questions that arise in the process of filling out the various forms. Our data suggest that both these efforts could have significant value in reducing administrative costs.

Other proposals for dealing with administrative costs address the problem more generally. Some involve the simplification of individual forms and the consolidation of several forms into one. Others involve checking to ensure that, as far as possible, the questions government asks correspond to the information that the businessman would normally gather for his own purposes. Our data suggest that these actions could be helpful as well, but there is the danger of increasing the complexity while reducing the amount of information required. Given the difference in cost to the business of the owner/manager's time versus that of others, the shorter, more complex form may not produce a net benefit. Several people we interviewed suggested to us that a concentration on lessening the burden on the owner/manager would be more effective than a more general effort at reducing reporting and record-keeping requirements, and our data strongly support that view.

Opportunity and Start-Up Costs

As mentioned before, opportunity and start-up costs are difficult to quantify because those people most affected are not around to tell their story. Nonetheless, the data do suggest some ideas. The major implication is that these costs are directly related to the uncertainty of government requirements. The responses to our questionnaire and the interviews we conducted showed a uniform tendency for fear of what may happen to be far worse than what actually does happen.

This distinction between perception and actions is very important, for it reinforces the point that attacking individual requirements one by one is a very inefficient way of achieving reform.

This "fear of the unknown" is not something that can be reduced by information alone. In fact, the information we have gathered suggests that a lot of uncertainty does exist. Although impacts of such things as license fees and inspections are relatively small in most cases, they can rise to dramatic levels in specific cases. For this reason, a little ignorance may actually reduce these impacts. Small businessmen may try new products or new locations or seek government contracts simply because they are not aware of the problems that have a low probability of occurring but tend to be severe when they do occur.

Of course, we are not recommending ignorance. Our analysis suggests that the best antidote to "fear of the unknown" is not ignorance but a feeling of control. Those small businessmen who had a sense that they could actually work with or around government (and there were a few who felt that way) were much more willing to deal with new products, move to new locations, or even start new businesses that others tended to avoid. Giving businessmen this sense of control obviously would not be an easy thing to do. Here again, we think the key will involve some form of collective private activity, but it will also involve some reorientation in the thinking and action of both business and government. A more complete discussion of this point appears in the next subsection.

One element of opportunity costs was particularly severe and thus deserves separate consideration. It involves the problems of doing business with the government. We encountered not few, but many, small businessmen who would absolutely refuse to pursue government business even when small business was guaranteed some advantage in the competition. The requirements in this area in particular can often be counterproductive. For example, one of the people we interviewed told us of a case where a general contractor could not get a particular job without signing up at least some minority subcontractors. However, all the minority subcontractors he contacted were not interested in doing work for the government because of the onerousness of the requirements. Such a situation is bound to lead to frustration and alienation and may even have a strong anticompetitive impact. If large businesses are able to jump through the hoops required to get the government's business, then they will thrive at the expense of the smaller firms. As for solutions to this problem, our data did not take us very far. In part, the reforms for dealing with this problem are no different than the reforms for dealing with other problems. In addition, however, government procurement represents such a potential for influence on the system that phase II should consider it carefully.

Cumulative Impacts

As noted previously, the collection of real impacts combines with fear to create a cumulative impact that is out of proportion to the specific "measurable impacts." Nonetheless, the problem is *serious* even when it is *not tangible*. Decisions not to hire new people or not to expand because government requirements interfere will have just as serious an economic impact as decisions not to hire new employees because the government requirement does not allow it. The most severe of these cumulative impacts is the deterioration in the relationship between businessmen and government; as a consequence, the most important reforms attempt to improve this relationship.

Addressing other costs with the reforms already discussed will deal with part of the problem, but not with all of it. Just as cumulative impacts are more than the sum of individual impacts, the cumulative reforms must be more than the sum of individual ones.

The reform suggestions we reviewed fell into three major groups. The first group attempted to create more direct contact between businessmen and government personnel. A watchdog group like the city of Seattle's Task Force on Small Business is a good example of this sort of reform.

The second group of reforms involved working to change government personnel's image of business. One suggestion, not at all facetious, was that those people who regulate a given business should be encouraged or required to take a course to learn about that business. The suggested courses in such a program would cover not just the technical aspects of the business operation, but also enough of the economic aspects to give the government regulator a fairly good idea of the pressures the businessman faces.

Of course, this would have to be done carefully. In many cases, the ideology that says "let's catch all the crooks" is a good one for at least some members of a regulatory agency to follow. Such an attitude guards against corruption. Even so, the attitude has to be tempered in some way if the two sides are to coexist better than they do now. Our research suggests that the reformer should work toward balancing the organization, not every single individual in it. The idea is to place within the government agency people who will play the same kind of watchdog and representative role that advisory groups play from outside the agency. A healthy tension at the lower levels of a regulatory agency will enable its leaders to obtain the kind of information or pressure that leads them to properly balance decisions. (In some sense our data suggest that businessmen should not fight government but join it.)

The final group of reforms addresses the problem of improving the businessman's image of government. Most of the ideas in this group involve some attempts to "personalize" government. The state of Michigan, for instance, runs advertisements showing one individual, with a short familiar first name, and a WATS telephone line that businessmen can call to handle their problems with the state. Other governments at various levels also have had success with this kind of approach. The basic idea could lead to some specific decision-making criteria. For instance, the Business License Center in Washington state could be faced with the choice between hiring an additional computer programmer so that its information is assembled better and processed faster or hiring a respected small businessman who would be more sympathetic and supportive of the people the office was trying to serve. Our data lead strongly to the choice for the businessman. Except in very specific instances, the problem an organization like the Business License Center should solve is not a technical one, it is a symbolic or psychological one.

Priorities among Reform Efforts

Since government requirements have many different kinds of impacts on small business, the question inevitably arises concerning which impacts deserve high priority in reform efforts. Our analysis does lead us to some conclusions on the matter of priorities. First, we found a very real distinction between psychological or symbolic impacts, on the one hand, and tangible impacts, on the other. The first set of impacts is definitely more important and deserves a higher priority in a reform effort. However, because at least part of the attack on the symbolic impacts is made up of attacks on many of the measurable impacts, some priority should be given to reducing these as well.

The data from our association survey, which have been discussed in Points of Views of Association Executives in chapter 7, provide a useful starting point. We asked the association executives to list the kinds of impacts that have the greatest effects on their membership. The result of these responses was a list, presented in the same section, that ranges from time spent on record keeping for government purposes to time spent on inspections. Record keeping and reporting headed the list, followed by direct compliance (referring to changes in physical facilities and work routines), information costs, opportunity costs, licenses and other fees, avoidance costs (such as challenges of a requirement), and inspections.

This ranking approximates our conclusions, with the following modifications:

1. The crucial element in the cost of record keeping and reporting is not the total time, but the time required of the owner/manager. Reform effort should be directed toward reducing the owner/manager's time, perhaps even at the expense of increasing someone else's time.

2. Direct compliance costs can be severe when they occur, but they tend to be unique to specific situations. Therefore, they are hard to address by general reform efforts. These costs are probably most significant for the fear that they generate. General reforms in this area will have to concentrate on reducing that fear.

3. The cost of information gathering is also most oppressive in terms of time of the owner/manager involved. This strain on the owner/manager is significant not only in a financial and business sense, but also in a symbolic one. Therefore, our research suggests that improving the flow of information is important, but the form in which raw data are delivered has to be given equal or greater importance.

4. Opportunity costs, like direct compliance costs, do not happen to everyone every year. However, the fear that they might happen is a constant one. Our analysis suggests that reform efforts should be addressed to the fear more than the specific impact. The fact that opportunity costs (which in this case include start-up costs) are number four on the list should not diminish their importance too much. Potentially at stake are more jobs and more new products, and consequently more new benefits, than are affected by any of the other impacts. The reason opportunity costs are lower on the list is that the reforms that address the higher items address these as well.

The danger in developing too definite a ranking of reform efforts addressed to tangible costs is that reform efforts could be led away from dealing with symbolic or psychological impacts, which are most important. The attitudes of business toward government and government toward business feed on each other. A vigorous attempt to eliminate a specific regulation because it requires a lot of record keeping, or to oppose one because it deals with a particularly dangerous pollutant, will do more harm than good if it leads to deterioration in the relationship between business and government. Consequently, any reforms addressed to specific measurable costs should be developed with regard to general impacts to ensure that they contribute to solving the overall problem.

Suggestions for Possible Reform Efforts

The best method of initiating a joint business/government approach to reform might be to first set up an advisory body composed of representatives from government, labor, associations, and small business. Special care should be taken in selecting the advisory group's size, composition of interest, and individual members. The ideal group might be a small board of leaders from the private and public sectors who are committed to designing reform efforts and positioned to act effectively in implementing those reforms. The composition of the group should fully represent the interests that would be affected by a reform program. An advisory group may function best under the auspices of an existing organization, such as Private Sector Initiatives or the Business Assistance Committee. If the advisory group is part of an existing organization, an effort should be made to involve other organizations that may play an important role in reform.

The role of such an advisory group would be, first, to define priorities for reform efforts, second, to identify and select an appropriate set of reform proposals, third, to allocate responsibility for the various reform efforts, and fourth, to monitor the progress of reform from conception to realization. Appropriate reform proposals based on the results of this study could be generated by members, by a review of reform proposals in other states or on the national level, and by the suggestions presented later in this chapter. Allocation of responsibility for reform efforts should use the unique strengths and expertise of appropriate public- and private-sector organizations. For example, the Association of Washington Business might be asked to spearhead a particular lobbying effort on the state level, the Puget Sound Council of Governments and the Puget Sound Chambers of Commerce could be approached for joint assistance in a series of local efforts, and so on. The ongoing monitoring function of the advisory group is important to orchestrate the overall reform program and to maintain a level of public awareness about its progress.

As an alternative, the advisory group might elect to deal with one reform effort at a time instead of attempting a large number of efforts simultaneously. This approach would have the advantage of concentrating the energy and resources of the group's members on implementing each proposal. Presumably the membership of the advisory group could evolve to include the appropriate interests in each reform effort it undertakes, while retaining a core of original members to maintain continuity and support.

Clearly, the formation of a joint private and public advisory group is only the first step in actively addressing the impacts of government requirements on small business. The most important function of an advisory group will be to design an effective reform program. Suggestions for possible reform efforts are presented in the next subsections.

Information: The Role of Associations

As pointed out earlier, the time and money spent by small businesses in gathering information can be one of the most costly impacts of government requirements. These "information costs" are exacerbated when the owner/manager is primarily responsible for researching requirements, especially when unnecessary frustration is added to an already time-consuming process.

Many small businesses are highly dependent on their associations for information about government requirements. Associations (and Chambers of Commerce) often possess the time and expertise necessary to keep abreast of regulatory developments affecting their membership. The information provided by associations is likely to be more seriously considered by small businesses, and associations are able to *interpret* requirements and provide a "sufficient" level of information (whereas government agencies may be forced to provide information more strictly "by the book"). By working to improve the system of information distribution, associations have the potential to reduce directly the information costs of government requirements to individual small businesses.

Any reform program working from the results of this study should take advantage of the unique strengths of an existing statewide network of associations and chambers of commerce to reduce the information costs of government requirements. This can be accomplished by improving the level and quality of information available to individual associations and by improving the system by which associations distribute information to their memberships.

Perhaps the best means of initiating such a process would be to hold a conference of associations, to exchange ideas and expertise on methods used to gather and disseminate information, and to discuss proposals for coordinating or streamlining the existing information system. Such a conference might profitably consider the following ideas:

Development of a model for association information services, including the best mix of services, and the best methods of acquiring and disseminating information. (Although most associations provide some type of information services, some are far superior in their methods.)

Methods for increased coordination of expertise among associations, allocation of responsibility for information on various areas of requirements, and mechanisms for information exchange.

Development of a private-sector central information clearinghouse as a backup service for small associations. Such a clearinghouse might best be housed within an existing organization (that is, through the Seattle or Puget Sound Chambers of Commerce, the Association Division of the Association of Washington Business, or an organization like the Washington Society of Association Executives). One activity of a clearinghouse might be to disseminate information to associations through a member subscriber service (including a single index of requirements).

Development of a training program or pamphlet to familiarize new association staff with information-gathering techniques.

Extension of the "employer consultant" concept to associations (government-sponsored employer consultants have been less than successful because of the reluctance of some owner/managers to submit themselves to possible enforcement actions. On-site inspections by an association "employer consultant" might be better received and lead to improved self-regulation within specific industries).

Proposals for improving the interchange of information between government agencies and associations with members affected by those agencies, and increased coordination among government agencies and appropriate associations in information distribution.

Incorporation of a curricular component on government requirements in existing management courses on small business (for example, those given by Seattle First National Bank and Rainier Bank in Seattle, seminars by the Puget Sound Chambers of Commerce, and university classes in business management).

Development of a reference pamphlet for individual businesses that could be distributed through the state small business office or through individual associations.

Information: The Role of Government

Although associations and chambers of commerce are probably in the best position to disseminate information to most small businesses, the government also has an important role to play in reducing the cost of information. Many small businesses rely on government agencies as their primary information source, and a large number of the smallest businesses may not belong to associations.

Government agency efforts to reduce information costs to small businesses should involve both improvement of information to individual businesses and improvement of information to associations with memberships affected by the agency's requirements. Special attention should be given to reducing psychological impacts, such as confusion, frustration, uncertainty, and so on, that can be caused by problems in the information and communication system.

A long-term improvement of government information may involve instituting a consolidated information system similar to the successful licensing information referral service. In the meantime, however, there are several appropriate government responses to the need for better information and communication with Washington state small business (many of which are already being instituted under the Business License Center and other agencies):

Designate specific staff members to answer all telephone inquiries within an agency or within a division of an agency. These staff members should be trained to (1) give clear, consistent information, (2) be sensitive to the attitude they project over the telephone, and (3) be directly familiar with any and all requirements for which questions may arise.

Issue a single index of types of requirements and corresponding agencies or divisions to all staff members designated to handle telephone inquiries. A small business owner/manager should be able to call a dozen agencies with the same question and be directed to the same person each time.

Institute an educational program to sensitize government personnel to the management perspective of a small business and the structure and processes of the industries that the particular government agency regulates; increase agency personnel awareness of the attitudes they project in their contacts with small business.

Expand the licensing information referral service to include federal and local licenses, permits, registrations, and so on.

Reporting and Record Keeping

A number of general suggestions are presented in this subsection to reduce the costs of filling out forms and maintaining records for government. Two general goals of reform efforts directed at government forms and records are, first, the overriding importance of reducing the time spent by the owner/manager, and second, the importance of reducing the frustration and "psychological burden" that many people feel when filling out government forms. Note that these are general suggestions based on our research, and several have already been instituted by various government agencies.

Forms that are sent to small businesses should first be pretested on a sample of small businesses.

Instructions should be included with forms (especially for explanation of particularly complex questions). In the case of frequent reporting forms, instructions could be in the form of a reference document to be consulted each month or quarter by the bookkeeper or secretary responsible.

Whenever possible, information requested by government forms should correspond to standard business records. In cases where special information is required, businesses should be informed ahead of time.

Reporting forms should be personalized by providing the name and phone number of the one contact person within the agency who is assigned to answer questions about a particular form or requirement.

Since a large majority of business reporting forms are sent to small businesses, *questions should be adapted to the scale and practices of small businesses.* In some cases, more detailed and complex forms could be sent separately to large corporations.

A reform program should especially consider methods of consolidating government reporting requirements. Such a consolidation would be a major administrative step and could be accomplished in a variety of ways:

Eliminate duplicate forms submitted to the same agency (especially important in government contracting).

Seek a consistent format among government forms required by different agencies (definitions and categories should be consistent; sequence of questions should be similar). Whenever similar information is requested, it should be requested in a consistent manner.

Explore the possibility of sharing information among different government agencies. Under this system, copies of a single form could be used by several agencies rather than each requiring a separate form. (Although there may be legal difficulties, the potential cost reduction could be significant.)

Expand the one-stop licensing program to additional industries (especially those with a predominant small business population).

Extend the one-stop licensing concept to local governments that have not yet adopted it.

The Small Business Task Force Concept

The city of Seattle Department of Community Development recently introduced an innovative approach to providing ongoing small business participation in the local regulatory process. The Mayor's Small Business Task Force is composed primarily of small business owner/managers from throughout the city and meets on an ongoing basis to consider issues of concern to local small business, especially problems involving local government requirements.

An ongoing advisory or watchdog group like the Mayor's Task Force is an excellent vehicle for improving communication between small business and government on the local level. Local agency personnel can become sensitized to the problems faced by small business, and the members of the task force are able to develop an understanding of the governmental process, which is essential in addressing reform constructively. The ongoing task force is preferable to an ad hoc political coalition because it emphasizes a conciliatory approach and members have a chance to study issues carefully before forming recommendations on proposed or existing requirements.

We feel that the small business task force approach has tremendous potential for providing small business input on the local government level, and local governments throughout the state should consider establishing similar groups. Based on the Seattle experience, special care should be taken in selecting a representative group of small business owner/managers to participate, and the task force should be structured as a constructive business/government partnership as opposed to simply a business lobby. Although the small business task force is best suited to the local government level, it might also be applied on a trial basis to individual agencies on the state or federal level.

Ideas for Future Research

As is often the case, this study has generated as many new questions as it has explored. Several of the more exciting research possibilities suggested by this study follow (some may actually be underway elsewhere now):

A study should be made of the validity and reliability of a sample of government forms. This study would use a sample of subjects typical of the small business personnel who usually fill out government forms. The sample would be divided into two or more subgroups. Each subgroup would fill out the forms using the same set of information. Comparison of the two subgroups would provide insights into the clarity and precision of the forms and would permit assessments of the likely degree of consistency of answers provided by businesses.

An attitudinal survey should be designed to further explore and trace the origins of the "psychological burden" discussed in this book. Such a survey could be conducted by a team of organizational psychologists and might use a sample group of both small business owner/managers and a random cross section of the population.

A detailed inventory should be made of government paperwork processed by individual businesses during a specified period. Each business would be carefully selected and subcontracted by the researchers to keep copies and fill out evaluations of each form, as well as to maintain careful records of time spent on government reporting and record keeping. Researchers would be responsible for training, monitoring, and processing results. The study could be repeated after a period of 4 to 5 years to evaluate growth or reduction in the total amount of time required to process government paperwork.

An analysis should be made of the sources and adequacy of the expertise available to small business in dealing with requirements. The present study suggests that one of the major problems is simply keeping track of new requirements. Analysis of the methods available to small businesses for doing so and the design of a demonstration program to improve these methods could be quite useful.

Appendix A:
Questionnaires

QUESTIONNAIRE TO SMALL BUSINESS OWNERS AND MANAGERS
ON THE COSTS OF GOVERNMENT REQUIREMENTS

Pages: 8 Estimated time to fill out: 45–60 minutes

We will treat the information you provide as confidential. You need not identify your company, except that it will be helpful when we are designing solutions to the problems identified.

Please feel free to attach your comments on a separate sheet if you need more space to answer a question.

A. COMPANY PROFILE

1) In which of the following areas of business activity is your company involved?

☐ Agricultural, forestry, and fishing   ☐ Wholesale trade

☐ Mining   ☐ Retail trade

☐ Construction   ☐ Finance, insurance, and real estate

☐ Transportation, communication, electrical,   ☐ Services
   gas, and sanitary services

2) What is your specific type of business? (e.g., motel, seafood processor, furniture wholesaler, etc.)

_____

3) When was your company established? _____

4) Average total number of employees: _____. If seasonal, indicate range: _____ to _____ .
    A) Number of "decision-makers" (partners, managers, assistant managers, etc.)_____.
    B) Number of "support staff" (secretaries, clerks, bookkeepers, etc.)_____.

5) Is your workforce unionized?

☐ Yes   ☐ No   ☐ Partially

6) Approximate annual gross revenue: $_____

7) Legal organization of your company:

☐ Single proprietorship   ☐ Franchise

☐ Partnership   ☐ Other:_____

☐ Corporation

8) Primary geographic area served:

☐ City or county   ☐ National

☐ Washington state   ☐ International

☐ Pacific Northwest   ☐ Other:_____

9) Other information related to size:

    A) Is your company owned by or affiliated with a larger corporation?
        ☐ Yes   ☐ No
    B) How many establishments (including headquarters) are maintained by your company? _____
    C) Do you report under IRS Subchapter S?
        ☐ Yes   ☐ No

10) What kind of access to legal expertise does your company have?

☐ Attorney   ☐ Attorney on   ☐ Attorney available   ☐ No special access to
   on staff   retainer   when needed   a particular attorney

11) What kind of access to accounting expertise does your company have?_____

12) Definition of small business:

    A) Do you consider your company to be a "small business"?
        ☐ Yes   ☐ No
    B) How would you define a "small business" in your industry?

_____

_____

B. IDENTIFICATION OF AGENCIES AND TYPES OF REQUIREMENTS

1) Requirements affecting your business

As far as you know, has a federal state or local government agency issued requirements in the following areas that apply to your business? If so, which level of government is involved. What level of impact do these requirements have on your business?

AREA	Any Agency Requirements That Apply?			Which Level of Government?			What Level of Impact?		
	Yes	No	Don't Know	Federal	State	Local	Light	Moderate	Heavy
Air pollution									
Water pollution									
Solid waste disposal									
Noise pollution									
Land-use/zoning									
Price of goods services									
Consumer safety/health									
Product safety									
Product performance/reliability									
Advertising/marketing									
Transportation									
Business Financing									
Employee safety/health									
Labor management									
Pensions									
Unemployment compensation									
Credit customer									
Energy use and rates									
Tax reporting									
Other:									

2) Which of the following government agencies has your business had contact with during the past year? What type of contact? How many times? Was the impact on your company light, moderate, or heavy?

FEDERAL (Check if contact)	TYPE OF CONTACT (SPECIFY NUMBER OF EACH CONTACT)					IMPACT
	Was inspected or investigated (inc. tax audits)	Filed a report	Applied for or re-newed a license or permit (inc. registration)	Ordered to comply	Received Information	1 - Light 2 - Moderate 3 - Heavy
Environmental Protection Agency (EPA)						
Consumer Product Safety Commission (CPSC)						
Food and Drug Administration (FDA)						
Federal Trade Commission (FTC)						
Occupational Safety and Health Administration (OSHA)						
Equal Employment Opportunity Commission (EEOC)						
Interstate Commerce Commission (ICC)						
Census Bureau						
Department of Transportation (DOT)						
Department of Health, Education, and Welfare (HEW)						
Department of Housing and Urban Development (HUD)						
Federal Energy Administration (FEA)						
Small Business Administration (SBA)						
Department of Agriculture (USDA)						
Securities and Exchange Commission (SEC)						
Other federal agencies:						
TOTAL ANNUAL CONTACTS						

STATE	TYPE OF CONTACT (SPECIFY NUMBER OF EACH CONTACT)					IMPACT
	Was inspected or investigated (inc. tax audits)	Filed a report	Applied for or re-newed a license or permit (inc. registration)	Ordered to comply	Received information	1 – Light 2 – Moderate 3 – Heavy
Department of Ecology						
Shorelines Management Board						
Forest Practices Appeals Board						
Attorney General-Consumer Protection Division						
Department of Labor and Industries (non-WISHA)						
Industrial Safety and Health Division (WISHA)						
Human Rights Commission						
Liquor Control Board						
State Employment Security Department						
Utilities and Transportation Commission						
Department of Agriculture						
Department of Revenue						
Department of Social and Health Services						
Department of Licensing (Includes business and profes-sional licenses-formerly Department of Motor Vehicles)						
Department of Natural Resources						
Other State Agencies:						
TOTAL ANNUAL CONTACTS						
LOCAL						
Building Department						
Health Department						
Zoning Board						
Fire Department						
Equal Employment Department						
Pollution Control						
Business Licensing						
Planning Department						
Consumer Protection						
Other Local:						
TOTAL ANNUAL CONTACTS						

3. Please rank federal, state, and local government in order of their "total impact" on your business: (1 – Least impact, 3 – Greatest impact)

   ☐ Federal   ☐ State   ☐ Local

4. Is your business affected by "Metro"? ☐ Yes   ☐ No

   If yes, please explain:_____

5. Is your business affected by government agencies in other states?   ☐ Yes   ☐ No

   If yes, please explain:_____

6. Which federal, state, and local government agencies listed above do you consider to have the greatest impact on your business?   Federal _____   State _____   Local _____

C. DIRECT COMPLIANCE COSTS

1) Licenses, Permits, Registrations and Filings (not including taxes).

   How many of the following are required of your business? What is the total annual cost?

	Total Number	Cost Per Year
Licenses/permits	_____	$_____
Registrations	_____	$_____
Filings	_____	$_____

B) If yes, please indicate the reason for each fine, the agency involved, the year, and the amount of fine.

REASON	AGENCY	YEAR	AMOUNT OF FINE

D. ADMINISTRATIVE COSTS

1) Inspections

A) How many man-hours per year does your company spend on government inspections? _____ hours per year

B) Which inspections take the most time? _____

C) Who is responsible for guiding or accompanying the inspectors? (Title or position) _____

D) How well do most government inspectors understand your business? _____

2) Reporting and Recordkeeping (not including tax forms).

A) How many man-hours per year does your company spend on filling out government reports? _____ hours per year.

B) Which reports take the most time? _____

C) How many man-hours per year does your company spend on filling out licenses, permits, registrations, and filings? _____ hours per year.

D) Which licenses, permits, etc. take the most time? _____

E) Have government reporting requirements caused your business to change or expand its existing recordkeeping system?

☐ Yes   ☐ No

F) What records do you keep primarily for government reporting purposes? _____

G) How many man-hours per year does your company spend on recordkeeping primarily for government purposes?

_____ hours per year.

H) Who is usually responsible for government reporting and recordkeeping? (Title or position) _____

I) What percent of the owner's or chief manager's time is spent on government reporting and recordkeeping? ____%

J) How many other people spend time filling out government forms and maintaining records for government purposes? What percent of their time is so spent? ____% each of _____ employees.

K) Have the administrative tasks associated with government requirements forced your business to hire additional administrative personnel?

☐ Yes   ☐ No   If yes, how many? _____

L) Approximately what percent of your company's administrative costs are attributable to government reporting and recordkeeping requirements? _____%

3) Miscellaneous Administrative Costs

Please estimate annual costs in the following categories resulting from government requirements:

Travel .... $ _____   New office space and office furniture ..... $ _____

Duplicating/Xeroxing .... $ _____   Data processing .... $ _____

Notary public .... $ _____   Overtime .... $ _____

Information distribution to employees ..... $ _____   Other: _____ $ _____

Storage Space .... $ _____   _____ $ _____

4) Overlap and Duplication

A) Are any of your business activities regulated by more than one agency or more than one level of government for the same purpose? (For example, federal, state, and local pollution or land-use controls)

☐ Yes   ☐ No   If yes, please identify: _____

B) Have you noticed any duplication in government inspections or reports?

☐ Yes   ☐ No   If yes, please explain: _____

C) Do government inspections and reporting requirements provide a steady, consistent administrative work load, or are they "bunched" at various times of the year, causing uneven demands on managerial and administrative time?

☐ Even load   ☐ Uneven load

Please explain (and specify times of year): _____

2) Work Routines

Has your business (since 1970) made any major changes in work routines (operating hours, retraining, etc.) to comply with government requirements?

☐ Yes   ☐ No   If yes, please explain:_____

3) Physical Facilities

A) Has your business (since 1970) made any major changes or additions to its physical facilities (new equipment, plant renovation, alteration of existing plant or equipment, etc.) to comply with government requirements?

☐ Yes   ☐ No   If yes, how many times?_____

B) In the spaces provided below, please describe each of the major changes required and estimate the total direct cost of compliance.

Type of change _____

Agency requiring change _____ year_____

Cost of managerial time spent to supervise and implement change: $ _____

Cost of employee time spent to implement change: $ _____

Cost of outside consultant or contractor: $ _____

Purchase price of new equipment or materials: $ _____

Increase in operating costs resulting from change: $ _____

Other costs: $ _____

Total direct cost: $ _____

Type of change _____

Agency requiring change _____ year_____

Cost of managerial time spent to supervise and implement change: $ _____

Cost of employee time spent to implement change: $ _____

Cost of outside consultant or contractor: $ _____

Purchase price of new equipment or materials: $ _____

Increase in operating costs resulting from change: $ _____

Other costs: $ _____

Total direct cost: $ _____

If your business had made more than two major physical changes to comply with government requirements, please estimate the costs on a separate piece of paper and enclose with this questionnaire.

C) How did you finance these changes?

☐ Bank loan   ☐ SBA loan   ☐ Retained earnings   ☐ Other:_____

D) Did you have any difficulty in obtaining financing to implement these changes?

☐ Yes   ☐ No

4) Equal Opportunity and Affirmative Action

A) Has your business (since 1970) made any changes in the following work practices to comply with Equal Employment Opportunity requirements?

Hiring?	Promotion?	Training?	Recruitment?	Layoffs?
☐ Yes ☐ No	☐ Yes ☐ No	☐ Yes ☐ No	☐ Yes ☐ No	☐ Yes ☐ No

B) Has your business (since 1970) faced a formal charge of job discrimination?

☐ Yes   ☐ No   If yes, how many times?

C) Has your business (since 1970) been required to award back pay or damages to any employee as a result of discrimination charges?

☐ Yes   ☐ No

D) How would you describe the impact of Equal Employment Opportunity requirements on your business?_____

_____

5) Disciplinary Fines

A) Has your business (since 1970) been required to pay any civil or criminal fines for alleged violations of government requirements?

☐ Yes   ☐ No   If yes, how many times? _____

E.   INFORMATION AND AVOIDANCE COSTS

"Information costs" result from the time and money spent trying to understand what is required by government. "Avoidance costs" represent the time and money spent in challenging or avoiding government requirements.

1) Information costs

A) Do you feel adequately informed about the nature and scope of government requirements as they apply to your business?

☐ Yes   ☐ No

B) Do you have any difficulty understanding what is required by specific government regulations and reporting forms?

☐ Yes   ☐ No

C) What percent of the time you spend on government reporting is taken up in trying to understand what is required by the forms?_____%

D) Which requirements or forms do you find most difficult to understand?_____
_____

E) What sources of information does your company rely on to keep informed about federal, state, and local requirements?

☐ Federal Register   ☐ Government agencies or personnel
☐ Code of Federal Regulations   ☐ Lawyer
☐ Wall Street Journal   ☐ Consultant
☐ Other business publications   ☐ Accountant
☐ Local newspapers   ☐ Union
☐ Trade association   ☐ Other: _____
☐ Business associates

F) Are you a member of one or more trade associations?

☐ Yes   ☐ No   If yes, how many?_____

G) How would you rate your trade association's performance in providing information about government requirements?

☐ Excellent   ☐ Adequate   ☐ Poor

H) How often have you required the services of a lawyer, accountant, or other paid consultant for information concerning government requirements?

☐ Never   ☐ At least once a year   ☐ 2-3 times a year   ☐ 4 or more times a year

2) Avoidance Costs

A) Have you ever challenged or appealed a government ruling or proposed regulation concerning some aspect of your business?

☐ Yes   ☐ No   (If no, go to Section F)   How many times?_____

B) Did your challenge(s) involve:

☐ Court hearing   ☐ Public protest
☐ Agency hearing   ☐ Simple refusal to comply
☐ Negotiation with agency personnel   ☐ Other: _____

C) Did you receive any help from other businesses or organizations?

☐ Yes   ☐ No   If yes, what kind of help? _____

D) What was the outcome(s) of your challenge(s) or appeal(s)?
_____

E) What would you estimate to be the total cost of your challenge(s) or appeal(s) (including legal fees, administrative costs, fines, etc.)?

TYPE OF CHALLENGE	AGENCY	COST	YEAR	DID YOU HAVE A LAWYER	
				YES	NO
1.					
2.					
3.					

F.   START-UP COSTS
(Do not fill out if company started before 1970)

In this section, we are seeking some measure of problems and costs associated with starting a business. We expect that these costs will vary depending on the type of business and the year the business was established.

1) Licensing, Permits, Registrations, and Filings

   A) Was your company delayed because of the existing licensing/registration/filing system?

      ☐ Yes   ☐ No   If yes, for how long? _____

   B) Did the delay affect your company's ability to obtain financing?

      ☐ Yes   ☐ No

   C) What was the direct cost of the initial licenses, etc.? $_____

   D) Did you have any difficulty finding out which licenses, etc. were necessary?

      ☐ Yes   ☐ No   If yes, please explain. _____
      _____

   E) How much of your (and your partner's) time was spent in obtaining necessary licenses, permits, and registrations?
      _____

   F) Was the relation between federal, state, and local procedures clear and consistent?

      ☐ Yes   ☐ No   Please explain.
      _____

2) Requirements

   A) Was your company required to comply with any requirements prior to operation? (For example, pollution control equipment, etc.)

      ☐ Yes   ☐ No

   B) If yes, what were the requirements and what was the cost to your company prior to operation?

Requirement	Cost
_____	$_____
_____	$_____
_____	$_____
_____	$_____

G. OPPORTUNITY COSTS

   Opportunity costs include those business activities which you chose not to undertake, which were delayed or cut back, or which you decided to stop as a result of government requirements or delays. Please check the activities affected by government requirements, what happened, and why.

ACTIVITIES AFFECTED	WHAT HAPPENED				WHY					
	Activity Never Begun	Activity Delayed	Activity Cut Back	Activity Stopped	Lack of Capital	Lack of Managerial Time	Government Delay	Complexity of Requirements	Cost of Requirements	Uncertainty over Requirements
Additional Plants or Offices										
Additional Employees										
Additional Product Lines or Services										
Product Development										
Expansion into New Geographic Markets										
Work under Government Contract										
Change in Location										
Property Development										

H. CUMULATIVE IMPACTS

In this section, please give your brief appraisal of how government requirements affect the following aspects of your business.

Price of goods or services	
Quality of goods or services	
Location of business	
Business growth	
Business profits	
Competitive position of your business	
Innovation	
Employment	
Relationship with employees	
Relationship with government	
Managerial independence	
Your "enjoyment" of doing business	

I. FOLLOW-UP QUESTIONS

1) Do you keep any record of government inspections, or of reporting forms sent to government agencies?

☐ Yes   ☐ No

2) Do you keep any record of time or money spent in complying with government requirements, inspections, or reports?

☐ Yes   ☐ No

3) OPTIONAL

Name of business _____

Address _____

Phone _____

Person completing questionnaire _____

Please feel free to add any additional comments, particularly about specific incidents involving government requirements.

QUESTIONNAIRE TO GOVERNMENT AGENCIES
AND DEPARTMENTS

1. Name of Agency or department: _____

2. Level of government

    ☐   Federal

    ☐   State

    ☐   Local

3. Name(s) and title(s) of person(s) completing this questionnaire:

    _____

    _____

4. Does your agency or department have <u>any</u> requirements (reporting, record-keeping, license/permit, inspection, or compliance requirements) which may apply to businesses in the state of Washington?

    ☐   Yes   ☐   No   If <u>No</u>, do not complete questionnaire.

5. What areas or consequences of business activity are regulated by your agency?

    1) _____

    2) _____

    3) _____

6. Which federal, state, and local agencies share your agency's jurisdiction over Washington state business?

        Agencies   Areas of Overlapping Jurisdiction

    1) _____   _____

    2) _____   _____

    3) _____   _____

7. Is there any formal or informal communication or coordination between your agency and those listed above?

    ☐   Yes   ☐   No

    If yes, please specify: _____

    _____

    _____

8. Identification of Requirements

Where applicable, please record information on those activities of your agency which affect Washington state businesses.

A) Report Forms Required as a Matter of Course

Form Name	Form No.	Purpose	How Often Required	When Required	Which Types of Businesses are Required to Fill Out Form?	Estimated Time in Man-Hours for Respondent to Complete Form

B) Reporting Forms Required in Special Circumstances

Form Name	Form No.	Purpose	How Often Required	When Required?	Estimated Time to Fill Out	Which Types of Businesses are Required to Fill Out Form?	Circumstances Where Required (Inspection, Special Emphasis, Etc.)

C) Additional Record-keeping Requirements

Record Name	Purpose (What is Being Recorded?)	Relation to Which Form Above?	How Far Back Is Record Required?	What Types of Businesses are Required to Maintain Record?	Estimated Annual Time To Maintain Record	Circumstances under which Data Recorded are Collected

D) Inspections or Investigations

Type of Investigation or Inspection	Purpose	Total No. per Year	Estimate How Often Each Business Is Visited	Average Duration	Under What Circumstances Does Investigation or Inspection Occur?	Announced or Unannounced

E) General Licenses and Permits (City and County Departments Only)

Name of License or Permit	Purpose	Annual Fee	How Often Required	When Required	What Types of Businesses Are Required to File Application	Circumstances Where Required	Estimated Time to Complete Application	Average Time of Government Response or Approval

9. Formulation of Requirements

A) As far as you know, is any special consideration given to the impact on <u>small</u> business of proposed requirements or procedures for your agency?

☐ Yes ☐ No

If yes, please explain:_____

_____

B) As far as you know, is there any direct participation by small business or representatives of small business in the consideration of proposed requirements or procedures for your agency?

☐ Yes ☐ No

If yes, please explain:_____

_____

10. Implementation of Requirements

A) Does your agency have any rules by which smaller companies are either exempted from or given special consideration in implementation of requirements?

☐ Yes ☐ No

B) If yes, please indicate these exemptions or special considerations below, including name of requirements and "size threshold" (company size standard affecting implementation):

	Name of Requirements	Size Threshold
Reporting	_____	_____
Recordkeeping	_____	_____
License/Permit	_____	_____
Inspection	_____	_____
Compliance	_____	_____

C) If your agency issues fines for noncompliance, are fines scaled to reflect company size?

☐ Yes ☐ No

11. Information Sources

   A) What information systems does your agency maintain to advise
      Washington State businesses of new and existing requirements?

      ☐   "Employer consultant"

      ☐   Public affairs office

      ☐   Direct mail

      ☐   Other: _____

          _____

          _____

   B) As far as you know, what sources do most small businesses rely
      on for information concerning your agency's requirements?

      ☐   Agency information systems

      ☐   Trade associations

      ☐   Newspapers

      ☐   TV and radio

      ☐   Word-of-mouth

      ☐   Other: _____

          _____

          _____

   C) Do you feel that small businesses under your agency's jurisdiction
      have adequate information about what is required by your agency?

      ☐   Yes   ☐   No

      If No, please indicate what practices you think might improve
      information distribution:_____

      _____

      _____

      _____

      _____

12. Impacts

    A) Which industries (types of businesses) are most notably affected by your agency in the state of Washington? (Please list in order of importance.)

       1) _____

       2) _____

       3) _____

    B) Which requirements of your agency (e.g., reporting, recordkeeping, inspections, compliance orders, etc.) do you feel impose the greatest monetary and time demands on Washington State small business? _____

       _____

       _____

    C) On an annual basis, approximately what percent of "cases" (including fines, compliance orders, etc.) are appealed or challenged by Washington businesses under your agency's jurisdiction? _____ %

    D) How would you characterize your agency's relationship with Washington state small businesses under its jurisdiction?

       _____

       _____

    E) What steps do you feel could be taken to improve this relationship?

       _____

       _____

    F) Do you have any suggestions for steps to reduce the costs of compliance with your agency's requirements?

       _____

       _____

    G) Please feel free to add any comments concerning the "impact of government requirements on small business," your reactions to this questionnaire, etc.

       Thank you for your time.

QUESTIONNAIRE TO ASSOCIATION EXECUTIVES

We are seeking information on the services provided by your association to help Washington state small businesses in understanding and coping with federal, state, and local government requirements. ("Government requirements" include all reporting, recordkeeping, application, inspection, and direct compliance requirements. Taxes and tax-related forms are not included.) Your responses will be kept confidential.

1. Association Profile

    A) Name of association: _____

    B) Name and title of person completing this questionnaire: _____

    C) How many Washington state businesses are members of your association? _____

    D) What is the average size, by number of employees, of your member businesses? _____

    E) What is the size range, by number of employees, of your member businesses? _____ to _____

    F) What percentage of your membership would you consider to be "small businesses"? _____

        What definition of small business are you using? _____

        _____

    G) Are your membership dues scaled to reflect business size?
        ☐ Yes   ☐ No

    H) Does your association specialize in a particular industry or industry group?
        ☐ Yes   ☐ No

    I) Does your association specialize in a particular area of business activity? (e.g., labor negotiation, marketing, etc.)
        ☐ Yes   ☐ No   If yes, please specify. _____

        _____

    J) What would you consider to be the primary functions of your association?

        1) _____

        2) _____

        3) _____

2. Information Services Relating to Government Requirements

    A) Does your association provide information about government requirements to its members?
        ☐ Yes   ☐ No   If no, go to Section 3.

    B) Which of the following kinds of information does your association provide to its membership?
        ☐ Often ☐ Sometimes ☐ Never - Inform members of federal legislative or regulatory developments.
        ☐ Often ☐ Sometimes ☐ Never - Inform members of state legislative or regulatory developments.
        ☐ Often ☐ Sometimes ☐ Never - Inform members of current legislation.
        ☐ Often ☐ Sometimes ☐ Never - Inform members of current agency policies.
        ☐ Often ☐ Sometimes ☐ Never - Legal advice to members
        ☐ Often ☐ Sometimes ☐ Never - Information on local legislative or departmental requirements.
        ☐ Often ☐ Sometimes ☐ Never - Other: _____

        _____

    C) Which of the following methods does your association use to disseminate information?
        ☐ Often ☐ Sometimes ☐ Never - Direct mail announcements.
        ☐ Often ☐ Sometimes ☐ Never - Association publications or newsletters.
        ☐ Often ☐ Sometimes ☐ Never - Phone calls to membership.
        ☐ Often ☐ Sometimes ☐ Never - Phone inquiries from membership.
        ☐ Often ☐ Sometimes ☐ Never - Membership meetings or conferences.
        ☐ Often ☐ Sometimes ☐ Never - Workshops on government requirements.
        ☐ Often ☐ Sometimes ☐ Never - Special handbooks on regulations.
        ☐ Often ☐ Sometimes ☐ Never - Distribution of published articles and reports on regulations.
        ☐ Often ☐ Sometimes ☐ Never - Other: _____

        _____

        _____

D) What methods does your association use to keep abreast of legislative and administrative regulatory developments affecting its membership?

1) _____

2) _____

3) _____

E) What methods would you propose to improve the quality of information you receive about government requirements? _____

_____

_____

F) Does your staff have expertise in any specific types of government requirements?

☐ Yes ☐ No   If yes, please identify your association's areas of expertise:

1) _____

2) _____

3) _____

G) What kinds of government requirements does your association need to know more about?

1) _____

2) _____

3) _____

H) What sources of information do most of your member businesses rely on for information about government requirements?

☐ Your association   ☐ Other business publications   ☐ Government agencies or personnel

☐ Other associations   ☐ Lawyer   ☐ Law reporters (for example, Environmental Law Reporter)

☐ Federal Register   ☐ Consultant

☐ Local newspapers   ☐ Accountant   ☐ Code of Federal Regulations

☐ Wall Street Journal   ☐ Union   ☐ Business associates

                                                       ☐ Other: _____

I) Do you feel that your members are adequately informed about government requirements which affect their businesses?

☐ Yes ☐ No

J) What kind of system(s) would you recommend to improve the level and quality of information on government requirements available to small businesses?

☐ Through an expanded role for individual associations?

☐ Through increased coordination of government-related activities among different associations?

☐ Through a state-run information office?

☐ Through a new federal department or federal "information locator" system?

☐ Through a central private sector clearinghouse for associations and individual businesses?

☐ Through a series of training sessions for association staff members?

☐ Other. (Please describe.) _____

_____

_____

3. Government Advocacy

A) Is government advocacy (testimony, negotiation, lobbying, etc.) an important priority of your association?

☐ Yes ☐ No

B) Is there a particular political action committee that your association works with?

☐ Yes ☐ No   If yes, please identify: _____

C) Which of the following advocacy activities does your association (or related political action committee) engage in?

☐ Often ☐ Sometimes ☐ Never – Testimony on proposed federal legislation.

☐ Often ☐ Sometimes ☐ Never – Testimony on proposed state legislation.

☐ Often ☐ Sometimes ☐ Never – Negotiation with state agencies on proposed requirements.

☐ Often ☐ Sometimes ☐ Never – Negotiation with federal agencies on proposed requirements.

☐ Often ☐ Sometimes ☐ Never – Legislative lobbying on state level.

☐ Often ☐ Sometimes ☐ Never – Legislative lobbying on federal level.

☐ Often ☐ Sometimes ☐ Never – Funding or participation in state political campaigns.

☐ Often ☐ Sometimes ☐ Never – Funding or participation in federal political campaigns.

☐ Often ☐ Sometimes ☐ Never – Testimony or direct litigation in state or federal courts.

☐ Often ☐ Sometimes ☐ Never – Drafting legislation.

☐ Often ☐ Sometimes ☐ Never – Drafting regulatory guidelines.

☐ Often ☐ Sometimes ☐ Never – Advertising or other public campaign related to regulatory requirements.

☐ Often ☐ Sometimes ☐ Never – Assist members in voluntary compliance with regulatory requirements.

☐ Often ☐ Sometimes ☐ Never – Monitor regulatory compliance of member companies ("self-regulation").

☐ Often ☐ Sometimes ☐ Never – "Regulatory problem solving" for individual members.

☐ Often ☐ Sometimes ☐ Never – Represent individual members at agency hearings.

☐ Often ☐ Sometimes ☐ Never – Represent individual members in court.

☐ Often ☐ Sometimes ☐ Never – Local government advocacy. (Please specify.):_____

☐ Often ☐ Sometimes ☐ Never – Other:_____

D) What suggestions do you have for improving small business representation in the legislative or regulatory decision-making process?_____

4. **Government Requirements which Affect Your Membership**

A) What are the primary industries represented by your membership? From your experience, which agencies and types of requirements have the greatest impact on these members?

INDUSTRY	AGENCIES	REQUIREMENTS

B) In general, are your members most concerned about federal, state, or local government requirements?

☐ Federal   ☐ State   ☐ Local

C) Which level of government is your association most actively involved in?

☐ Federal   ☐ State   ☐ Local

D) If your association receives information requests about government requirements, what kinds of information are most often requested?

1) _____

2) _____

3) _____

E) How costly to your members are the following types of government compliance? (High relative to other types of compliance, moderate relative to other types, or low relative to other types.)

☐ High   ☐ Mod.   ☐ Low – Direct compliance costs (to change physical facilities, work routines, staff, etc.).

☐ High   ☐ Mod.   ☐ Low – Time spent filling out government forms.

☐ High   ☐ Mod.   ☐ Low – Time spent on record keeping for government purposes.

☐ High   ☐ Mod.   ☐ Low – Time spent on inspections.

☐ High   ☐ Mod.   ☐ Low – Time spent gathering information about government requirements.

☐ High   ☐ Mod.   ☐ Low – Money spent on professional advice (lawyers, accountants, etc.).

☐ High   ☐ Mod.   ☐ Low – Time and money spent challenging or appealing government requirements.

☐ High   ☐ Mod.   ☐ Low – Disciplinary fines.

☐ High   ☐ Mod.   ☐ Low – License/permit/registration fees.

☐ High   ☐ Mod.   ☐ Low – Opportunities foregone due to cost or complexity of government requirements.

☐ High   ☐ Mod.   ☐ Low – Other (please specify): _____

_____

_____

F) What currently proposed or possible future regulatory developments cause you the most concern? Why?

1) _____

2) _____

3) _____

G) From your experience, do you feel that there is a qualitative difference in the problems faced by small business (as opposed to large business) in dealing with government requirements?

☐ Yes   ☐ No   If yes, please explain: _____

_____

_____

_____

H) Please describe any existing strategies or ideas you have for reducing the costs of compliance with government requirements. _____

_____

_____

_____

Thank you for your time. If you have further comments or questions, please let us know.

Appendix B:
Analysis of Hypotheses
Generated from the
Literature Review

The literature review was particularly helpful in generating a number of hypotheses about why government requirements might impose more severe problems on small businesses than on large ones. In this appendix we present a number of those hypotheses, together with some discussion of their validity based on our data. The hypotheses and comments are grouped by cost category.

Direct Compliance Costs

1. Small businesses have less capital available to pay the monetary costs.

Comment: The lack of capital appeared to be important when the smallest firms were required to make physical changes. It was not a major factor otherwise among the firms we studied.

2. A disproportionate share of their available capital must be devoted to "non-productive" compliance costs as opposed to "productive" product development, expansion, and the like.

3. Small businesses must pay higher interest rates for short-term loans, further restricting the available capital.

4. Small businesses have such a small share of any market that they cannot pass through cost increases to buyers the way businesses with a larger share of the market can.

5. Many compliance costs, such as license fees and fines, are regressive; they are either the same for all businesses or they do not decrease proportionately with business size.

Comment: Many agencies have taken steps to make their fees and other requirements less regressive; some agencies even have schedules of fines.

Administrative Costs

6. There are significant economies of scale in all forms of administrative overhead that give large businesses an advantage; because government-imposed requirements do not vary proportionately with business size, small businesses

must devote a greater share of their administrative resources to complying with government requirements.

Comment: Our data did *not* show that the smallest firms had the greatest percentage of overhead devoted to government requirements. Moreover, the percentage of overhead devoted did not increase proportionately with business size.

7. Reporting forms and requirements are often geared to the management, production, and record-keeping systems of larger companies.

Comment: We did not find any forms geared to larger businesses, but owner/ managers made this comment in our study.

8. Small businesses often lack the data-processing capacity, standardization of procedures, and specialized staff that larger businesses possess.

Comment: The lack of specialized staff was definitely a major problem.

Opportunity Costs

9. Small firms are more likely than large ones to lack the expertise required to find the least costly ways of achieving compliance with government requirements.

10. Government requirements divert the managerial resources of small firms more than those of large firms because such resources are limited in small businesses.

Comment: Our data definitely support the hypothesis that government requirements divert more managerial resources in small firms than in large ones, although the differences might not be as great as some literature implies.

11. Small businesses have smaller cash flows, so they are less able to cope with extended marketing delays.

12. Small businesses in general operate in a system of greater risks, and probably smaller returns to risk, than large businesses do; government requirements increase those risks.

13. Government requirements increase with any change in size, location, market, and/or production; as a consequence, the requirements constitute disincentives to growth, mobility, and innovation.

Comment: Our data suggest that the fear that new government requirements may accompany business changes is more important than the requirements themselves. The fear does constitute a significant barrier to innovation and expansion.

14. Government requirements constitute significant barriers to entering a new market; they add to the needs for expertise and capital because they involve many licenses and permits, together with long delays in obtaining those licenses and permits.

Comment: We found that government requirements constitute a barrier to new businesses in some specific cases but not in others. A barrier tended to exist in innovative industries, such as aquaculture.

15. Government requirements are more numerous and more severe for firms doing business with the government. As a consequence, many firms, particularly small ones, feel that a sizable market is closed to them.

Comment: Government requirements were a significant barrier to doing business with the government, especially in construction. Here again, the expectation of trouble was just as important, if not more so, than the actual experience of it.

16. Government requirements add to the research and development costs needed to introduce a new product. Therefore, new firms are less likely to start and existing ones are less likely to expand.

Information and Avoidance Costs

17. Small firms are easier targets for regulatory enforcement than are larger firms. The larger firms have greater access to the legal and political resources needed to resist enforcement.

18. Small firms have less access to regulatory decision making and political activity in part because they have fewer resources to devote to such activities and are less willing to get involved.

Comment: Our interview data supported the hypothesis that small firms are less involved in political activity. However, our survey of small business owners uncovered many who were quite active politically. The hypothesis may be true in general, but it is at least subject to numerous exceptions.

19. Small firms are more likely to react after the imposition of a requirement than to act before the requirement is imposed. Large firms are more likely to know of impending government requirements.

20. Small firms pay disproportionate fees for outside expertise, such as legal advice, because obtaining expertise is also subject to economies of scale.

Appendix C:
Selected Case Study
Interviews

Electronic Equipment Manufacturer

This company is a medium-small electronic equipment manufacturer. The manager, who oversees government compliance and receives, handles, and routes most government reporting forms, described government requirements in terms of level of government:

1. Three city governments with jurisdiction over the company have requirements relating to licensing, fire and building, and so on.
2. Counties are involved with building permits and conditional use permits for some of the company's electronic installations.
3. METRO (a special district in King County, Washington with responsibility for sewers, among other things) is primarily involved in chemical wastes from the plant, resulting in a sewer service charge.
4. State and federal (see discussion).

All mail goes first to the manager (Mr. X). Special reporting forms are handled directly by him. Routine tax and employment forms are routed to the bookkeeper. Inspections are handled by the foreman or the manufacturing vice-president.

Mr. X said, "Our contacts are very routine, actually," except for contract requirements.

The government is a customer, but the company does not actively seek government contracts. In general, the manager does not find government requirements to be a major problem, and his company does nothing substantially different for government customers. The major problem with government customers is that they are slow to pay bills. (King County: 30 days; Seattle: 30 to 90 days; some state and federal agencies: 90+ days). Another problem with doing government work is that there is no one to talk to in government who knows what is going on.

Mr. X related an amusing example of the "Pandora's box" of some government contract work. Several months ago less than $50 worth of electronic equipment was sold to Phoenix, Arizona, and last week the company received a reporting form from Phoenix on the company's Affirmative Action Program that requested $250 dollars worth of information.

Mr. X said that the EEO form would take 10 to 15 hours a week and that related requirements would entail major changes in work routines, so they are planning to limit the number of employees. To hire more than the ninety-nine employee cutoff for EEO would require hiring of an additional employee for record keeping and the luxury of a government relations staff. Mr. X said that the Seattle cutoff point for EEO of four plus employees was not being enforced because of lack of funds. The company's only past problem with Affirmative Action involved a charge that was eventually thrown out but which took a lot of managerial and legal time.

Major reporting/record-keeping problems involve FCC (maintaining records for customers) and the formulation of the company's ERISA plan in 1974, which created enormous legal and accounting costs.

Mr. X said that the general requirements of WISHA and the fire department are "nothing you wouldn't do yourself," and that his estimates of compliance costs did not include those compliance costs which "make sense."

Mr. X said that he has to gather his own information because he has no specialized staff to advise him. He is always looking for new information. His best information comes from "boardroom reports," Research Institute of America reports (including special reports and alerts), and trade journals, but "there is no way you can know all the regulations that apply to you." His accountant also does a lot of advising, especially on government financial requirements. Mr. X says that to run a business you need to read a lot. His company is also a member of seven separate associations with expertise in the various activities conducted by his company. Mr. X says that he reads between fifty and sixty reports, newsletters, and so on per month relating to new information on government requirements.

Mr. X praised the Research Institute of America reports which he called much better than the Commerce Clearing House and other regulation reporters because they are generalists and not agency-specific. He also seeks information requirements from his lawyer once every 2 months and from his accountant once a week. Probably as a result of his incessant search for new information, Mr. X says he *does* feel adequately informed about government requirements which apply to his business. He said that for essential information on government requirements he would recommend the *Kiplinger Report* and *The Wall Street Journal*. For deeper information Mr. X felt that the Research Institute of America approach was excellent and had saved him much time and effort in the past. Mr. X felt the role of the trade association should be to identify specific requirements applicable to specific lines of business. He felt that the Association of Washington Business did a good job on general requirements and said that as far as he knew there were few businesses that were not "associated," and he could not understand how a small business could survive without association information.

In Mr. X's experience, government agencies have been quite good about supplying information. The major initial hurdle is to find out which agency to call, especially on the city and county level. Mr. X says that business owners must recognize that government is here to stay and learn to cope instead of fight. Mr. X said that he had expected to report a very high destructive impact before he filled out our questionnaire, but in going through our questions, he really could not find it—he ended up feeling better than when he started.

Chemical Manufacturer

This company is a manufacturer, retailer, and wholesaler of chemicals. The average number of employees is thirty-three, with a small factory and two retail/wholesale outlet stores.

The decisionmakers in this company include the president, the sales manager, and the office manager. The office manager, Mr. X, is responsible for most of the work related to government requirements. All government reporting forms come directly to his office, where he collects information from the chemists, warehouseman, and so on, compiles it with the help of the bookkeeper and the CPA (especially for tax purposes), and sends the information back to the appropriate government agency.

Some of the areas of requirements which have a heavy impact on this firm are consumer safety, transportation, employee safety, and pensions. In this case, *heavy impact* means requirements, or reporting forms, which are especially *time-consuming*.

In the area of consumer safety, requirements related to product labeling were called "phenomenal." To verify label ingredients, this company must sometimes run its products through an independent lab at added expense.

In the area of transportation, the Department of Transportation (DOT) regulates the packaging of chemicals (hazardous materials and so on). The major problem in this area is that changes or additions to regulations are so frequent (on a monthly basis) that the office manager has a very hard time keeping track of what the current regulations are.

The area of employee safety has an essentially high cost impact on this company because of the toxic chemical nature of the products handled by its employees. Requirements to install showers, sprinkler systems, and so on have added substantially to this company's overhead as a nonrecurring direct compliance cost.

In the area of pensions, this company was forced to drop its profit-sharing plan because of the high cost of government-required outside accounting. Prior to 1976 this company had in-house accounting, but "the government in effect outlawed it." According to Mr. X, everything relating to profit sharing and pensions was presented by the government in terms of an implicit adversary relationship between the business and the employees. Finally the business and the employees made a joint decision to drop their profit-sharing pension plan, because "it was doing no one any good."

The company formerly registered products with the Environmental Protection Agency, but certification would often take more than a year, which they could not afford. Since the U.S. Department of Agriculture has a much faster approval system (6 to 8 months), the company switched registration of its products from EPA to USDA. Mr. X said he had noticed some "turf" dispute between EPA and USDA on the issue of toxic chemicals. He said that there were also similar problems between FDA and USDA/EPA. He said that these three agencies lacked well-defined boundaries in the area of chemical regulations.

Mr. X could remember five specific examples of changes to the company's physical facilities. Most have taken place at the manufacturing plant, with three of these changes being environmental-related: an $8,500 filtering system for chemical tanks was required, $8,000 worth of ground preparation work, and $8,000 to build a moat around a chemical tank farm. The two other major changes were safety-related, involving complete sprinkler systems and protective showers for employees as well as special bathroom facilities. The total cost of the safety-related requirements ran between $3,000 and $4,000. Miscellaneous employee safety equipment (boots, gloves, ear and eye protection, filtering systems, and so on) has also been required.

Mr. X said that most government inspectors do not really understand what the product is that his company produces. This is especially true in contracts with the government; inspectors come to inspect the individual product or just to collect samples but they do not know anything about what the product is used for. Auditing also creates special problems. Different auditors often require different accounting procedures. Mr. X feels that the lack of coordination between different government agencies, especially in the area of inspections, is one of the major problems facing small businesses. He felt that if inspectors understood the business they would not be as strict.

Mr. X also felt that government-related record keeping is much more expensive than people generally thought, because of the storage space, computer time, and numerous ancillary charges and costs that are normally not taken into account.

At this point, the company has completely given up on government contract work. It is often impossible to find out exactly what is required, and it is extremely difficult to meet both specifications on the finished product and specifications on individual ingredients. He says it becomes a matter of product quality: "There are people in the business that can cut corners more than we are willing to." Additional requirements associated with a government contract can cut the thin bid margin for smaller companies.

The best information sources for this company are the Association of Washington Business (AWB) for general information and federal specifications from the GPO bookstore for specific information. Trade associations in this industry are still in their infancy, and their information on government requirements is "no help at all." AWB provides good general information, but "the main problem is filtering out information that is useful to you for your business." Mr. X also gets some information directly from the agency involved, but oftentimes he has run into government personnel who either do not know what the regulations are or who contradict themselves and other agency personnel.

For example, he once called the Department of Transportation and talked to someone who had not even read the regulations he was asking about. He has learned not to take anyone's word over the phone. He wants all information and requirements from the agency in black and white. He says that there is a similar lack of information and contradictory information at the Internal Revenue Service.

This company has been involved in three direct challenges to government rulings. These have included a property tax assessment, a DOT packaging requirement, and a joint attempt by the company and its employees to "do away with the union." (In this case, Mr. X claimed that it was harder for his employees to get out of the union than to get in initially.)

The major opportunity costs of government requirements for this company were found in the area of product development. The company hired a chemist 2 years ago to develop a line of chemicals for a certain industry. Twenty products were submitted in sequence to the USDA, and after a year and a half, only eight of those products had been approved. Unfortunately, however, a partial line of products cannot be sold effectively to an industry. Product development is already such a costly and time-consuming process that the additional costs and delays of government registration take away all remaining incentives for product development: "It all boils down to where you want to spend your time—we have given up on product development." In the last 6 to 9 months, many of the registration requirements have changed, and even to get their eight registered products reapproved will take 6 to 9 months. In fact, he even expects a substantial delay in getting his company's existing products relabeled. ("As far as government is concerned," the label is as important as the product.)

He also complained about Oregon's competitive advantage over Washington state in the area of taxation and freight tariffs.

Mr. X felt that government requirements have actually strengthened his company's relationship with its employees. He said that a camaraderie had developed between the employees and the business, because the employees identified with the problems that the business faced in its dealings with government. Employees especially identified with taxation problems of the company, and many government regulations are often questioned first by the employees themselves.

Photographic Laboratory

This company is not severely impacted by government at this point, but looking at the experience of similar companies elsewhere, the president, Mr. X, expects that OSHA/WISHA and EPA are likely to become bigger problems in the future. He hopes that enforcement of these laws will depend on the reasonableness of the appropriate inspector.

The company's major regulatory expense at this time involves a Department of Licensing review of its profit-sharing plan. The cost of lawyers may run into thousands of dollars. Mr. X said that the review could have a big impact—because employee's money cannot be used for business. It is *untouchable* money.

The company is a subcontractor to several large corporations and also has a GSA contract from the government. Therefore, it has many EEOC requirements from these contractors, even though it is a relatively small operation.

All government-related documents, information, and so on go directly to the president, except for routine tax forms, which are sent to the CPA. The office manager handles the records for tax and payroll information and prepares information for the CPA. The CPA prepares the tax reports. Mr. X does all the other types of reports. Three percent of gross sales goes to the CPA. Seventy percent of the office manager's time is spent on government reporting and record keeping. Inspections and audits for state revenue and sales tax have been made four times in 4 years. Audits take all the time of two people for 1 week.

Mr. X said that "most people don't think of ancillary charges" when computing administrative costs. Thirty percent of this company's administrative costs go to government requirements in the form of rental, forms, and other miscellaneous administrative costs.

Mr. X called the Research Institute of America his "best source of information."

Mr. X is very active in his associations and in local politics, and he has taken out-of-pocket trips to Washington, D.C. to testify and negotiate for industry. He feels that "one of the biggest shames in this country is the tendency of a lot of small businessmen not to be involved in politics. . . . It's foolhardy to say I'm too involved in the business to worry about politics."

Mr. X also criticized the completely adversary relationship between business and government and wants to work against the common belief that business is the villain: "What you're damning is the little guy when you're damning business." (The real villain is larger business.) Mr. X particularly objected to the distrust implied by repetitive cross-checking questions on government forms.

Mr. X thought that many businesses avoid speaking out because of the possibility of "spite inspections and government retaliation." At the moment, Mr. X is simply waiting and hoping for the best, relying on the possibility that his company may be too small to attract regulatory notice.

In closing, Mr. X repeated his major point about the lack of political involvement among small business owners: "If a majority of businessmen realized how simple it is to get equity from their elected officials, they would end up doing it more often. . . . If they take the time to do it, we would have a far better business climate."

Engine Parts Wholesaler

Administratively, this company has a fairly loose organization, with four key decisionmakers and four other managerial personnel. Managerial tasks are usually grouped by the functional areas of the company.

One partner now works primarily in government sales, which accounts for between 10 and 20 percent of current business. An employee in the export department handles most of the regulatory matters pertaining to government contracts. She has become an expert on EEO requirements, drafting the EEO plan, supervising hiring, screening, and so on, and acting as personnel director. Inspections (up to 50 hours per year) are usually handled by the general manager. Auditing and routine reports are handled by the bookkeeper. Mr. X noted that "we come under all the requirements everyone falls under." The company's revenue is so high that they are not exempt from any requirements, and there is no difference in regulatory implementation between them and the major corporations.

This company has had repeated problems with the state Human Rights Commission. Mr. X said that it is difficult when the government flaunts its authority continually. He objects to having power so concentrated in individual government representatives, who cannot do their job without "rubbing your nose in minority rights." Mr. X feels that his company was singled out because of an isolated incident of over 1 year ago in which the company had attempted to fire an unproductive minority employee, who quit and filed a discrimination charge. Mr. X summarized the Human Rights Commission's handling of the case by saying that it is "inconceivable that it could happen in the United States." He said that during the hearing the activist representative of the Human Rights Commission had put him and his associates down continually, assuming that they were lying. The case has been dragging on for 2 years now at a cost of $20,000 plus managerial time. Mr. X said that this money has been spent solely to make a point, and that the amount of money actually disputed is 3 days of unemployment compensation. Mr. X said that he objects to the treatment he has received as a person and to the attitude of government, the abuse of authority, and so on. Mr. X said that he believes in standing up for his rights and has challenged government rulings many times in the past, especially in cases of false claims for unemployment compensation and disability payments.

"We're too small to be big and too big to be small." Big business regulations apply especially to government contract work and interstate sales. This company does not have enough staff and administrative overhead to adequately handle proliferation of government requirements it routinely faces. Mr. X said that government regulations for small businesses are "pretty damn tough," especially in inflationary areas such as highly finished steel. A small company cannot build capital because of inflation and government requirements.

Mr. X is especially concerned about the possibility of future noise pollution requirements in industry and is already making attempts to reduce the noise levels in his plant. He does not know where his company stands in relation to consumer safety, but he is very concerned about product liability.

In terms of reporting, Mr. X had particular objections to census reports. He objected to having separate census reports for separate establishments with the same parent company. He also said he must make ridiculous guesses on many of the census questions ("Its typical of government forms not to give you enough categories").

Electrical Contractor

This company is a medium-small electrical contractor engaged in industrial and commercial work, with employees on various job sites around Puget Sound, Washington state and the Pacific Northwest. All employees are union employees. The company is divided into six departments, each of which has a separate manager who works out of the main office. Each manager is responsible for preparing budgets, hiring, payroll, and so on. In addition to the six department managers, there is one general manager who oversees the entire company. All government forms come through the main office, and each department manager fills out his own forms.

The company is especially notable for the amount of government contract work it does. Last year over 80 percent of this company's work was on government contract. On the average, this company contracted with ten federal agencies, six state agencies, three county agencies, and five city governments. Ms. X, the office manager, noted that there is duplicative paper work with each contract, which has the effect of raising office overhead. Reporting associated with *federal* contracts is by far the most difficult and time consuming for this company, demanding longer and more frequent reports. An example of duplicative paperwork on the federal level is that ten separate copies of the same EEOC report must be filed for each of ten federal contracts. Among the worst federal reports are the certified payroll reports and the EEOC reports.

The most excessive and duplicative reporting requirements occurred on projects that involved a combination of federal and local funds. Ms. X gave an example of a joint contract which was administered by a local city. The city had originally told this company what forms were required, but at the end of the project, a federal agency demanded a set of forms that the city was not aware of. Ms. X said that this situation was especially burdensome because the additional reporting was not included in the initial cost estimates, and that it was even more time consuming to go so far back in the records instead of having filled out the reports on a monthly basis throughout the project.

Ms. X says that she recently received nine calls from Washington, D.C. concerning reports filed on the same job. A different person called each time.

It seemed to her that not one of them knew that the others were calling. She also has discovered that a lot of government employees do not even know what their own requirements are.

Ms. X criticized the government's tendency to come on much too strongly at training sessions on how to fill out government forms. She finds this offensive, and at the same time it reduces her motivation to fill the forms out correctly.

Among federal agencies, the Navy has been the most complex and time consuming in terms of reporting requirements.

According to Ms. X, the reporting forms and instructions for the "certified payrolls" do not correspond to the information requested. She finds it literally impossible to fill them out, and she says that the government personnel are very particular about how these certified payrolls look, but that they do not really care what the information is. Also, although the government uses computers, they will not accept a computer printout. She could not see the reason for this and felt that it has needlessly added to her company's overhead.

She also questioned the requirement for so many government reports during a project. She noted that when a contract is signed, the company is required to fill out an "affidavit of compliance" relating to stipulations in the government contract. She feels that this should be enough, but the government is naturally distrustful of business and continually investigates, doubts, questions, and assumes the company is trying to cheat.

Government contract requirements are routed through the office in the following way. The department head initially checks the specifications and distributes them through the office manager to the estimators, purchasing agent, various clerks, and the "man in the field." After distribution, the specifications are returned to the office manager and then finally back to the department head. After the initial routing of government specifications, most of the reporting is handled directly through the main office.

Ms. X felt that the costs associated with the government reporting, record keeping, and so on come out to be much higher than the 2 percent of administrative costs that she reported on the questionnaire. Although it was hard to estimate hours per week spent on government forms (because government-related reporting and record keeping are divided among the six support staff in the office), she concluded that if all government-related reporting and record keeping were concentrated on one person, that person would spend at least 40 hours a week on government forms (including payroll and tax forms).

Ms. X has always wanted to keep an ongoing record of the cost of government reporting and record keeping, but she has never had time. "It's such boring work...if it just had some significance. It costs more and it doesn't bring any more efficiency."

EEO requirements have an impact on all phases of hiring and firing, promotion, training, recruitment, and so on. This company has had problems in the past because "we hire through the union so we don't have much say so about who is hired." An effort is made to ask the union for minorities, but the final decision is often up to the union. She said that minority employees are often hired for a specific job, but are kept on if there is work to be done. More training has been required since the advent of EEO requirements because less-qualified people are coming into the job. Often minorities come on line without a full apprenticeship, and training must take place directly on the job site. This company has faced one formal charge of discrimination involving a layoff of a minority employee. This case involved an eventual settlement.

An example of lack of communication between agencies on EEO requirements occurred about 1 year ago. The company bid for a job on the city level and was called by the local EEO officer, who asked about the minority representation among the company's employees. The company told the EEO officer to wait and see if they received the contract and then to call back. The EEO officer said that would be no contract without prior compliance. This was contradicted by a phone call to the contractor.

Reporting requirements tend to be bunched at the end of the fiscal year to an "outrageous" degree. Infrequent periodic reports with no advance warning of what will be required are perhaps the most burdensome and time-consuming, because the office staff has to go back through records up to 1 year old and must construct some records that were not kept originally.

As the office manager, Ms. X was not very familiar with inspections that took place on the job site, but she noted that once every 6 weeks there is a safety meeting on each job site.

A repeated complaint about government requirements was that no one in government knows what the requirements are. There is no coordination between agencies: "I wish you could call someone and get a packet."

This company has challenged government requirements several times. These challenges have included a challenge to part of the National Electrical Code, minority set-aside, and failure of payment by a government agency.

But there has never been any feeling that government work should be avoided: "You do government work because it is a major part of the economy." She said you have no choice and you simply have to adjust.

Ms. X said that government technical employees are very well qualified, but that the bureaucrats dealing with government paperwork really do not understand what is going on in the field.

She noted a reluctance of many small subcontractors to participate in government work, because they did not have the kind of office staff that her company employed. She noted that it becomes especially difficult to recruit minority subcontractors required by EEOC for this very reason.

Moving and Storage Company

The receptionist greeted me at the door by saying "Are you from an agency?"

The manager, Mr. X described his business as a typical moving and storage company, with five full-time employees and five part-time seasonal workers when volume is heaviest (from May 15 to September 15), working exclusively in moving and storage (household moving primarily).

Considerable rules and regulations govern the moving and storage business, especially the federal agencies ICC and DOT. As agents of a national van line, this small company is required to abide by ICC regulations. The national company publishes customized reports for its agents detailing government requirements and paperwork violations. It receives ICC and DOT reports from the individual agents and forwards them to the appropriate agency. These reports include DOT drivers' logs and numerous annual and monthly reports for the ICC. The purpose of the report to agents is as a "self-improvement report card," and the national company does not directly penalize its agents for fines or violations.

Mr. X receives the DOT log forms from a local printer and the ICC reporting forms directly from the ICC. The Washington Utilities and Transportation Commission reports are received directly from WUTC for work in Washington state. State reports are handled solely in the company's office and sent directly back to the state agencies. The manager's role in government reporting involves routing to the bookkeeper or other appropriate administrative personnel and reviewing the reports before they are sent back to the state agency. The bookkeeper is responsible for filling out and keeping government-related records.

The manager is responsible for guiding all inspectors. One day last month four inspectors came to the company at once. They were from the local fire department, a military base, the Military Traffic Management Command, and the Washington Utilities and Transportation Commission. Most recent government problems have involved the WISHA inspection of 3 months ago, prompted by the high back injury rate in the moving and storage industry. The WISHA inspector made a thorough inspection, which lasted more than 2 hours, and found three violations (swing saw without a guard, elevator platform without a railing, and lack of three-prong electrical outlets). This company spent $1,000 on renovations for the one major and two minor violations. "The funny thing is none of the violations related to the industry's injury rate," complained Mr. X. Finally, the Washington Utilities and Transportation Commission sends two separate inspectors, a paperwork inspector and a warehouse inspector. The longest inspection is the WISHA inspection, which generally takes 2 hours, plus another 2 hours for a visit from the employer consultant. Other inspections usually take 30 to 60 minutes. "It seems like there are more inspections now—they like to come unannounced."

Mr. X talked at length about ICC rate-setting procedures, saying that sometimes his company lost money on certain routes. He said that it was difficult to plan for cost versus revenue, but that ICC rates guarantee a reasonable rate of return if the business is managed properly.

Seventy percent of this company's moving and storage work is done under contract with the Department of Defense. Numerous contracts apply to different types of moving and storage. Mr. X complained about ICC Section 22 Filings, which allow moving and storage companies to bid lower than the going

ICC rate for government work. Also, state agencies get an automatic 20 percent reduction from the ICC rate. Competitive bidding is also prevalent on the city and county level. Mr. X felt that this system was unfair to the individual customer: "If we could set all jobs at the same rate, we could charge the individual a lower price."

Annual government contracts are handled through the various base procurement offices. Contracts are based on type of shipment and destination. With regard to government contract storage, you have to file a low rate or meet the low rate to get any business at all. The going "low rate" is one-third of the ICC rate. Although there is not a lot of additional reporting and record keeping required for government contract work in moving and storage, there are additional costs that are not reflected in the lower prices charged to government users. These costs include information costs associated with numerous compliance requirements. I was shown several thick booklets of requirements for transportation, travel, and traffic management regulations that apply to government contract work. Mr. X said that it was extremely difficult to "catch" some of these requirements on his own. An example of contract-related requirements resulting in opportunity costs was the so-called 2-inch requirement, mandating that storage platforms to be raised 2 inches off the ground. This requirement appeared after flooding in warehouses around the country last year. This company's platforms were only $1\frac{1}{2}$ inches off the ground, and as a result, the company lost $2,000 to $3,000 in government business and had to renovate its warehouse, which is located on a hill.

Information sources for this company include the local government procurement office, information briefs from the national company, government inspectors, and four moving, storage, and warehouse associations to which this company belongs. The best information comes directly from government, especially in contract work. Trade associations are especially good at explaining regulations in comprehensible language. Mr. X showed me a trade association's translation of a recent "notice of proposed rulemaking" as an example of the type of information his company receives.

Glass Installation and Service

Mrs. X called her three-person company "small enough so we can't get federal help, big enough so we can't get welfare." She felt that government requirements had a low impact on her glass installation and service business at all levels. The most problems she has had with government requirements related to the hiring of a single employee. In addition to standard employment security requirements, she was required to make a $500 deposit on the employee with the Department of Labor and Industries, based on the assumption that the employee would work out of doors.

In terms of administrative time spent on record keeping, the Department of Revenue (DOR) quarterly reports hit the hardest; records must be kept on geographic area served, which she often finds difficult because of hazy city and county geographic boundaries in her area. She claimed that "all of my bookkeeping is basically done for the government." She said that she spends $\frac{1}{2}$ hour a day plus a full day per quarter on DOR forms alone. The only duplication she has noticed is in the area of unemployment tax forms. Although the company is not heavily impacted by government requirements, at this time, Mrs. X voiced some concern about new requirements of the Consumer Product Safety Commission (CPSC) involving safety glass. She says that she generally spends 10 to 15 minutes on the phone talking to each customer explaining government regulations on safety glass. She said that the insurance does not pay for it, building inspectors do not enforce the standards, the builder does not want it, and in the end the glass company is the only one who is really accountable and liable.

To gain information on these requirements, her partner went to a safety seminar on the new CPSC safety glass requirements. In general, information on requirements is obtained directly from the source: "If I am really stumped I call the government." In the past, her information requests of government have met with excellent success.

Homebuilder

"So what can I tell you about government paperwork?" said Mr. X as we sat down in his office. His company is a land development firm that also runs a real estate division and a building division. They build 200 to 220 houses a year. Mr. X considers that the right amount, good for any market conditions. The company develops and builds in three Washington state counties. In all, the total employment range for the company is between thirty-nine and fifty. Mr. X said that the different divisions were set up for administrative and union purposes.

One of the biggest problems of the homebuilding industry is the frequent fluctuation of the market. This company's goal is to employ people steadily and not to fluctuate with the market.

All administration and government paperwork is handled through the central office. Inspections take place on-site and are handled by foremen in the field.

Mr. X thought it best to discuss government requirements in the chronological sequence of building a house or development. He said that at the land-acquisition phase, there is the most involvement with government. This involvement includes

1. The preliminary plat: This document must show that the development will meet all requirements for engineering, sewer, water, power, streets,

and so on. The company must hire an engineer to prepare all the preliminary plats for public hearings (the city or county agency may also decide that an environmental impact statement is necessary). The preliminary plat applies to all land development over four house lots.

2. The company must deal with the local water district, sewer district, and power company, including liaison work, familiarity with differing local requirements, and personal contact with district personnel.

3. The third major area of government regulation in the land-acquisition phase involves FHA specifications for housing open to customers with government loans.

Mr. X says that complying with FHA requirements is a matter of choice, in order to expand the market—the reasoning is that if the market dries up, there will still be FHA money. "But there is a whole raft of builders who won't put up with all that paperwork."

All the preceding requirements, including preliminary plats, water and sewer requirements, and FHA paperwork, must be submitted and applied for before construction can begin. Mr. X said that most of the current problems in developing are at the county and city levels. Delays can range from 6 months to 2 years, which means that the land development company must remain 2 years ahead on lot supply. Local delays are the result of political philosophy rather than paperwork problems. For government agencies, delays are an "easy out" when faced with no-growth political pressure, and "delays are continuous and repeated." Mr. X summarized the impacts of government requirements in the land-acquisition phase as follows:

Plats—long political delays.

Water and sewer districts—managerial time expended in liaison work (and information gathering on differing requirements of the various district jurisdiction).

FHA—substantial paperwork.

Mr. X said that his partner does most of the hearings/liaison work and that they also hire a company that specializes in such liaison work. This subcontractor represents the developer in local hearings, keeps an ear to the ground for potential problems, and so on. Without this outside company, Mr. X estimates that his office staff would have to be increased by two to three people simply for liaison and local government work in the initial application stage.

Mr. X described the preparation of plats as follows: the engineer provides technical information to the staff, which compiles and routes the application. Mr. X said that the initial paperwork was not too onerous and was negligible in the overall picture when compared with time delays and lack of predictability in government actions.

After the preliminary plat has been developed and approved, the company also must apply for a building permit with the city and the county. Time spent is 1 hour per permit plus 3 to 4 additional hours of the staff architect's time (keeping plans in order, keeping track of changes in local building codes and FHA specifications and changes). One permit is required per house. Also, an FHA conditional permit is required for each house, including an FHA appraisal, which often comes out too low and must be challenged three to four times, causing substantial time delays. The company also obtains a similar permit from the VA, which is far less time-consuming than FHA permits. Mr. X was critical of the FHA bureaucracy—he said that there were many dedicated people in the agency, but little overall organizational coordination and direction.

After all the initial plans and permits are developed and approved, construction may begin. The primary impact of government in the construction phase involves the first, second, and final inspections.

The first inspection, by the county or city, occurs after the foundation is laid. At this point, there is also a first inspection by the FHA. After the first inspection, house construction proceeds relatively uninterrupted until the second inspection stage. At this point, the house is structurally complete, before any interior finishing is begun.

The second inspection takes about an hour per house in contrast to the much quicker first inspection. "I don't want you to get the impression I think that's a bad hour—good inspections are a good thing." "We have the staff to deal with this—a lot of those guys don't—and I don't want them to get away with anything." Mr. X noted that there was very little paperwork during the construction phase. All government contacts took place by phone or in person. Between the second inspection and the time the house is complete, the only contacts with government relate to subcontractors, who often have to get permits for an individual job and order their own inspections. This does not impact the company directly, except occasionally in time delays.

When the house is complete, the final inspection for occupancy is made, by both the city/county (for code requirements) and the FHA (for code requirements and general "workmanship"). The biggest problem for homebuilders in this last stage is code interpretation. From time to time different inspectors interpret the code differently, occasionally causing time-consuming and costly changes. After the final inspection, the city approves the house and signs off the permit, and the FHA gives final approval for sale.

In the meantime, the real estate division of this company has been developing a relationship with potential buyers. The impact of government requirements on these retail activities is minimal in comparison with problems in the land development phase. First, sales are indirectly impacted by truth-in-lending laws affecting mortgage brokers. Second, the Moss-Magnuson Warranty Act directly impacts real estate sales (the FTC interpreted a house to be a consumer product, requiring simple language and a clearly defined dispute-settlement procedure on all house warrantees). Mr. X said that he estimates 1 hour of a salesman's time per customer per house is spent in explaining warrantee requirements in compliance with this act. Third, the company must sign an initial agreement with FHA to try to market houses to minorities. This agreement includes preparation of a "marketing plan" for FHA, which must be updated twice a year (20 plus hours). Monthly record keeping is also required for FHA, to report the number of potential minority buyers that visit the property (4 to 5 hours per month record keeping).

Mr. X summarized the impact of government requirements on his retail division as follows: "So our dealing with the customer in buying a house isn't greatly impacted by federal paperwork . . . except when he goes in and applies for a loan, but you can talk to the banks about that."

Mr. X said that there were several types of requirements that applied to on-site work routines, but that these were also minimal in comparison with government requirements in the land development phase. First, an EEO plan is required to do FHA work. This affects the company as well as its subcontractors. The number of hours worked by all employees with a breakdown by race is required. He estimates that each subcontractor spends 3 hours per month on EEO reports, all of which are sent back to the general contractor's office for compilation, which generally takes about 6 hours per month. Mr. X said that he could only remember one WISHA inspection. He said that WISHA does not generally concern itself with the residential building industry, but that some subcontractors are impacted separately. Mr. X said that if his company were required to meet all the specific safety and health requirements, "It'd be a can of worms." Finally, work routines are also impacted by the local air pollution control agencies, which required permits for burning on-site.

Mr. X said that little managerial time is spent on reporting and record keeping, but that managers do spend a lot of time on government liaison work, "putting out fires", and so on. He could not provide an accurate estimate of administrative costs due to government requirements and said that the problem was limiting the category: "We interface with government on so many levels . . . that it's hard for me to sort it all out."

On the subject of information costs, I first asked Mr. X what I would have to do if I wanted to get into homebuilding. He laughed and suggested the following: buy predeveloped lots, get an outside CPA, get a good insurance agent, talk as much as you can to other builders, make a lot of contacts with developers and subcontractors, and start *small*!

Mr. X said that the proliferation of requirements has been incredible in the last 11 years (since this company was started). Initial approval once took only 90 days, there was only a first inspection, and there were no FHA requirements. "We could build a house in 50 days. . . . Now that time is 90 days, [but] I don't want you to feel that I'm a proponent of going back to the old system, because I'm not." Mr. X said that the impact of government requirements on homebuilding was proportional to the number of units, and that since a permit was required for each house, a plat for each development, and so on, there is no informal cutoff point in terms of company size for government impacts.

Mr. X said that he gets his best information from the Association of Washington Business, lenders and banks, and his own staff's specialization. He said that most builders have outside realtors who deal with government requirements for them. The structure of his company has improved the amount and quality of information, because the expertise is all within the company and there is greater coordination and communication.

In terms of proposed or recent requirements, Mr. X was very apprehensive about the proliferation of energy-related insulation requirements at the state, local, and federal levels. Many of these requirements conflict with one another, and many do not fit in with standard building practices. Mr. X felt that there were going to be a lot more regulatory mistakes in relation to insulation and energy in the next several years. Mr. X also noted frequent changes in the Uniform Building Code, which is amended yearly at the federal level and is accompanied by state and local amendments at the same time. Mr. X pointed out that the committees meet once a year to "amend the code," and therefore the code keeps getting amended and the costs keep going up.

Impact largely depends on government personnel. An example of a bad government employee is one who provides no information, keeps you guessing, and maintains an adversary relationship with the business, trying to "catch you." Mr. X said that his company tries to avoid hostility at all costs. They try to find a person within the government bureaucracy and talk to him or her personally, obey the directives, and avoid a confrontation relationship. But Mr. X also noted that "as much of that attitude is a result of the businessman as of the government employee," and "I think one of the biggest problems with government requirements is in your mental attitude."

In closing, Mr. X emphasized the use of paperwork as a political tool. He said that paperwork is as difficult or as easy as the agency that is interpreting wants to make it. "Most people want to comply with the law, but if you can't do it, the law is too complicated."

With regard to tax laws, Mr. X said that "I was trained as a CPA, but now I have to hire outside CPAs to handle the present tax laws."

Wholesale Growing Nursery

This company originally included several retail establishments, which were dissolved, largely to reduce the amount of regulations and because of the feeling of the partners that with twenty-five to thirty employees their business began to be susceptible to unionization. The company is still a corporation, but it is now much smaller, not so exposed to various state and federal regulations.

Mr. X, the owner/manager, handles all government-related reporting and record keeping, except for routine business reporting such as tax forms, payroll, and so on, which are handled by the bookkeeper. Mr. X estimates that 20 percent of his time is spent on government-related work. Government reporting tends to be "bunched" at the end of the year, at which point it becomes a full-time job.

Mr. X said, "I don't mind some of the reports, it's just the nature of the questions." He said the government asks questions that are very difficult for a small company to answer. The worst offenders in this regard are census reports and ERISA reporting, where many of the questions apply to large companies, but are very difficult for a small company because so many functions are under the jurisdiction of the owner/manager.

Mr. X was highly critical of the government's general lack of accessibility. Once, to clarify a series of questions on a ERISA form, he called repeatedly to Seattle and was unable to get anyone on the phone. He concludes that "It's a one-way communications system: *Down*!"

Several examples were used to illustrate what Mr. X called "a level of incompetence which is astonishing in our state and local government." The first example involved a diesel pickup truck owned by the business. Mr. X was told that he needed a permit to operate the diesel vehicle and was given a lengthy Washington state pamphlet on diesel vehicle regulations. However, no one was able to tell him exactly what the procedure was to get the permit and he ended up losing a whole work day with a trip to Olympia to deal directly with the agency people involved. Another example, relating to workmen's compensation, is a good example of government delay. An employee at the nursery filed for workmen's compensation after breaking a foot on the job. Three weeks later nothing had happened, and after repeated phone calls from the owner, the state could not locate the application and requested a refiling. Two weeks later there was still no response: "By the time this boy got paid, 6 weeks later, he was already back to work. . . . We were the ones who bailed him out. It's really a sad commentary."

Another example of problems with workmen's compensation involves the recent state law that gives corporate state officers automatic coverage under workmen's compensation. Because of this law, Mr. X's personal insurance rates jumped from $28.00 a person to $324.00 a quarter for three people. He called this a "flat ripoff" because workmen's compensation coverage begins only when the salary stops. This is ridiculous when applied to small business owners, an example of a "hidden law" that slips through in a larger piece of legislation. He claims that many state legislators did not even realize what they were signing.

"I don't know about anybody who's happy doing business anymore." "I used to work for somebody else—I made a lot more money. Now I just have my independence and a lot of hassles with government."

Mr. X said that the heaviest government impact on the state level was due to the combined efforts of the Department of Agriculture and the Department of Ecology in relation to insecticides, fungicides, and so on. He said that several years ago three people at this company were licensed to use insecticides, fungicides, and so on, on the various plants in his wholesale greenhouse. He thinks that this licensing process was generally a good thing and that he and his employees learned to respect the chemicals after taking the required courses.

But now he has been told that his company will incur a liability unless they get new separate licenses to spray specific chemicals on specific types of plants. In other words, instead of a single license for a single chemical, each chemical will require separate licenses for each individual type of plant species. The Department of Agriculture has told him that they will not enforce this particular law, but that the company would be held liable in case of a customer complaint or lawsuit.

Mr. X also noted that it was unclear in his business where Department of Agriculture jurisdiction ended and Department of Ecology jurisdiction began. Other Department of Agriculture requirements include a yearly license and an inspection one to three times a year.

An example of inflexibility in local government requirements occurred in a recent landscaping job at a local shopping center. A design was originally presented to the planning department, and later in the implementation of that design, a few minor changes in shrubbery were made with the approval of the planning department. The company then received a call from the Public Works Department; the department demanded that the company remove certain shrubs that might eventually block the sidewalk. At this point, the developer called the mayor and "raised hell." The Public Works Department continued to demand removal of the shrubs because they were not on the original design plan. Finally, the Public Works Department was forced to withdraw its demands after being unable to find a regulation that specifically prohibited the shurbs from blocking the sidewalks. Mr. X said that this was an example of the lack of communication between different government agencies and showed how government does everything by the book, everything by the plan, without any flexibility at all.

All inspections are handled by one of the partners or managers. Longest inspections are the local boiler inspection (one-half day) and the State Department of Agriculture inspection, which usually lasts 2 to 3 hours. The biannual state sales tax audit is particularly burdensome.

Mr. X's best information on government requirements comes from trade publications. He has no satisfactory rapport with any government agency and receives very little useful information from government. He is a member of three industry-specific trade associations as well as AWB. He finds the AWB monthly newsletter to be very helpful and praises AWB for being "instrumental in flagging proposed regulations of interest on the federal and state level."

Mr. X noted two types of opportunity costs used by government requirements. First, the area around this company's nursery has recently been zoned residential, which in effect boxes in the company and prevents future expansion. Second, he has found that he cannot hire high school summer help anymore because the minimum wage does not justify it. He has been forced to upgrade and reduce his number of employees, and he is no longer taking on any temporary help.

Appendix D:
Analysis of Businesses Responding to the Mail Survey

Types of Businesses Responding

The eight categories listed in question 1 (area of business activity) were drawn directly from SIC industrial divisions. Question 2 asked respondents to write in their specific type of business. These answers were subsequently coded by two-digit SIC "major group." Responses to both questions were then regrouped by industrial divisions, because many answers were inconsistent. We assumed this inconsistency stemmed from unfamiliarity with the SIC coding system. Consequently, we relied on the specific question (2) rather than the general question (1) when the two were inconsistent. A large number of respondents checked two or more areas of business activity in the first question and listed several types of business in the second question. This supports the hypothesis that many small businesses are highly diversified, engaging in several market areas simultaneously (that is, a small manufacturer engages directly in whole-sale trade and distribution or operates a retail factory outlet). Multiple responses were identified by primary activity (usually listed first). The percentage response of respondents by SIC division is listed in figure D-1. This distribution is roughly parallel to the distribution of small business firms in Washington state as revealed by the Dun and Bradstreet data (see figure D-2).

Several more specific types of businesses had relatively larger numbers of responses. Two-digit SIC major groups with ten or more responses are ranked in table D-1 as a percentage of all responses.

Types of businesses with five to nine responses (less than 3 percent of total responses) are listed in table D-2.

The most notable characteristic of the top five groups is their inclusiveness, which helps to account for the higher number of responses. Also, in the category of special trade contractors, most of the responses were received from electrical contractors (partially because of an additional mailing through the Seattle Chapter of the National Electrical Contractors Association), and the category of "wholesale trade—durable goods" may include a number of trucking firms (which could account for the relatively low percentage of respondents—2 percent—in the "motor freight transportation and warehousing" category).

There was a disappointing lack of response in several industries identified by the SBA as having high percentages of small business establishments, sales, and employees nationwide. The low number of responses in these categories may reflect either a low government impact or, more likely, a low membership

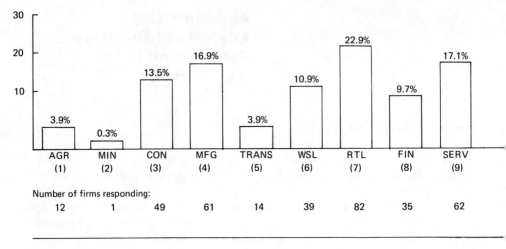

Figure D-1. Percentage Distribution of Respondents, by Industrial Division.

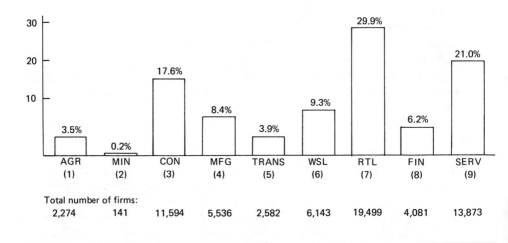

Figure D-2. Percentage Distribution of Washington State Businesses with less than 50 Employees, by Industrial Division (Calculated from Dun and Bradstreet Data).

Table D-1

Responses by SIC Major Group, for Groups with Ten or More Responses

SIC Major Group	% of All Responses
Construction	10
Miscellaneous retail	10
Wholesale trade—durable goods	9
Business services	5
Automotive dealers and gasoline service stations	5
Insurance agents, brokers, and service	4
Fabricated metal products, except machinery and transportation equipment	4
Machinery, except electrical	3
Apparel and accessory stores	3
Miscellaneous services	3

Table D-2

Responses by SIC Major Group, for Groups with Five to Nine Responses

SIC Major Group	Number of Responses
Automative repair, services, and garages	9
Building construction—general contractors and operative builders	8
Lumber and wood products, except furniture (manufacturing)	8
Motor freight transportation and warehousing	8
Furniture, home furnishings, and equipment stores	8
Agricultural production—crops	7
Construction other than building construction—general contractors	6
Wholesale trade—nondurable goods	6
Building materials, hardware, garden supply, and mobile home dealers	6
Banking	6
Miscellaneous repair services	6
Real estate	5
Personal services	5

in the organizations that distributed the questionnaire. These industries include hotels and motels (two responses), eating and drinking places (one response), and amusement and recreation services (one response).

Employment Size of Respondents

Responses to question 4 (average total number of employees) ranged from "none" to over 1,000, with most of the responses falling in the range of fifteen employees or less (median = 15.214). Approximately 81 percent of respondents reported fifty employees or less (the state of Washington definition of a small business), with approximately 10 percent of respondents falling within the thirty-five to fifty employee range.

In some cases, respondents indicated a range of employment rather than an average total number of employees. In most of these cases, the mean of the range was selected to represent the average total number of employees. The experience from most of the case studies indicates that the numbers of decision-makers and support staff listed are also included in the average total number of employees. It is also interesting to note that responses are clustered at multiples of five (that is, 10, 15, 20, 25, and so on). In some cases, this clustering may be related to certain size cutoffs (especially for the ten cases clustered at fifty employees) for government assistance or enforcement, but it is more likely that these figures were selected as rounded-off estimates.

Respondents are grouped in figure D-3 into eight employment-size categories (clustered at the low frequencies), which are roughly comparable to categories used by various federal, state, and local organizations to define small business. Figure D-4 shows roughly comparable data for the state as a whole. The respondents contain fewer tiny businesses (zero to nineteen employees: 55 versus 89 percent) and more intermediate and larger businesses. The respondents do contain enough cases to suggest the range of impacts in the smaller sizes, but the differences in percentages suggest that extrapolations of averages to the state as a whole should be made very carefully, if at all.

Average Gross Revenue of Respondents

The approximate annual gross revenue (question 6) ranged from $16,000 to $60 million (two uncoded responses were above $100 million), with most of the respondents reporting at or below $1 million annual gross revenue

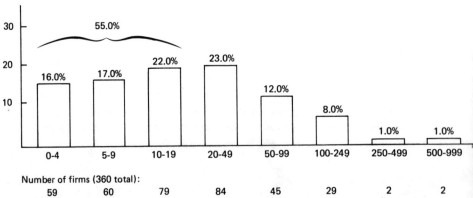

Figure D-3. Percentage Distribution of Respondents, by Number of Employees.

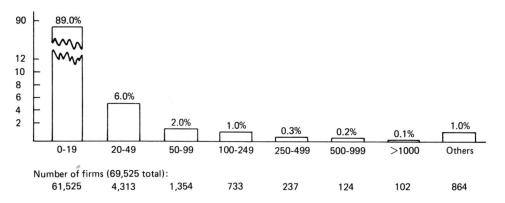

Figure D-4. Percentage Distribution of Washington State Businesses, by Number of Employees (Calculated from Dun and Bradstreet Data).

(median = $999,929). As in the case of employment size, responses were clustered at rounded numbers (especially at $100,000, $500,000, $600,000, $1 million, $1.5 million, $2 million, $2.5 million, and $5 million). Approximately 30 percent of respondents reported between $0.5 million and $1.5 million annual revenue. In figure D-5, respondents are grouped into seven size categories.

The categories generated in this section (major industrial division, number of employees, and revenue size) have been used to analyze the distribution of responses to each of the important questions in the small business questionnaire. Responses were first reviewed for all businesses, followed by a summary of variation from the standard response by six major industrial divisions. (Because of a shortage of responses, divisions A, B, and E will be noted only where a strong and consistent tendency exists.) We also describe variations in response by size categories and variation in response by selected two-digit SIC major groups.

Relationship between Respondent Size and Industry

Table D-3 illustrates the distribution of respondent number of employees by major industrial division. The results of this cross-tabulation are not surprising, reflecting the range in median size expected among the various industries.

The relationship between respondent size and industry is important to remember when evaluating data from the small business questionnaire; that is, what may appear to be an industry-specific type of impact may actually be associated more closely with size, and vice versa.

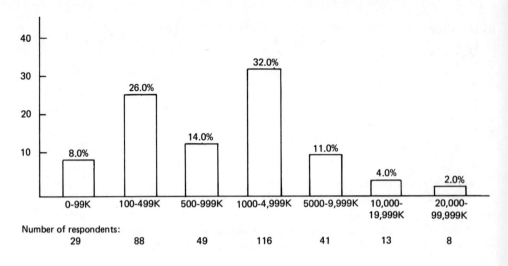

Figure D-5. Median Annual Gross Revenue of Respondents, in Thousands of Dollars.

Table D-3
Number of Respondents, by Number of Employees and by Industrial Division

	All Businesses	Number of Employees						
		0-4	*5-9*	*10-19*	*20-49*	*50-99*	*100-249*	*250-499*
All Businesses		59	60	79	84	45	29	2
Agriculture	12	–	1	3	3	3	2	–
Mining	1	–	–	1	–	–	–	–
Construction	49	14	1	9	19	3	3	–
Manufacturing	61	5	3	7	17	14	13	1
Transportation	14	1	0	7	3	3	–	–
Wholesale	39	2	7	8	12	7	2	1
Retail	82	14	22	20	18	4	4	–
Finance	35	7	9	6	5	6	2	–
Services	62	13	17	17	7	5	2	–

Note: Row totals and column totals do not always equal sums of the appropriate cells because the totals include businesses that did not specify number of employees or industrial division.

Bibliography

Published Articles

Albouy, M. 1975. Economic regulation in business. *Mgt. Int. R.* 15(1):107.

Allen, G. 1977. Growing resistance by small business. *Am. Opinion* 20 (May):31-54.

*American Enterprise Institute for Public Policy Research. 1977-1978. *Regulation* (entire series).

*Bauer, G.L. 1977. Fighting government regulation: Who says you can't win? *Assn. Mgt.* (October):49-60.

Benham, Lee and Alexandra. 1975. Regulating through the professions: A perspective on information control. *J.L. and Econ.* XVIII(2):421-447.

Copulos, M.R. 1977. The costs of regulatory agencies! *Mich. Challenge* 17(2):8-11.

Cunningham, W.H., and Isabella, C.M. 1976. Consumer protection: More information or more regulation? *J. Mkt.* 40(2):63-68.

Duncan, J.W. 1975. Seeking reductions in the federal paperwork burden. *Statist. Rep.* 76 (July):1-11.

Ford, G.R. 1975. The impact of regulation on our economy. *Mich. Challenge* 15(7):5-6.

Gillette, D. 1977. How regulations encourage and discourage innovation. *Res. Mgt.* 20(2):18-21.

Goldberg, V.P. 1974. The economics of product safety and imperfect information. *Bell J. Econ.* (Autumn):683-688.

Googins, R.R. 1977. Developments in state regulation—A panel. *Bus. Lawyer* 32(Spring):855-867.

Grundy, R.D. 1976. The impact of federal regulation. *Challenge* (November-December):34-52.

Hall, H.R. 1975. The tyranny of overregulation. *Mich. Challenge* 15(7):7.

Harper, J. 1977. Toward a more rational analysis of state action exemption of antitrust law. *Louisiana Law R.* 37(4):949-956.

Henderson, H. 1973. Ecologists versus economists. *Harvard Bus. R.* (July-August):28-36, 152-157.

Holmberg, S. 1975. Regulation Q and consumer protection—Legal and economic guidelines. *Bank. Law J.* 92(10):1073-1097.

Horton, F. 1977. Cutting red tape for small business. *Nat. Pub. Accountant* 22(April):11-16.

Hyatt, J.C. 1975. Strangling in red tape. *Wall St. J.,* October 13.

---

*Particularly useful references are highlighted by an asterisk.

International Council for Small Business. 1977. Government regulations (special issue). *J. Small Bus. Mgt.* (October).

Jordon, W.A. 1970. Product protection, prior market structure, and the effects of government regulation. *J.L. and Econ.* 15(1):151-176.

Kelman, S. 1974. Regulation by the numbers—A report on the consumer product safety commission. *Pub. Interest* (Summer):83-102.

Kobelinski, M.P. 1976. On the future of small business. *Nat. Pub. Accountant* 21(November):8-13.

*Kristol, I. 1975. The new forgotten man. *Wall St. J.* (November 13):20.

*Leone, R.A. 1977. The real costs of regulation. *Harvard Bus. R.* 55(6):57-66.

*Lilley, W., III, and Miller, J.C., III. 1977. The new "social regulation." *Pub. Interest* 47(Spring).

Magazine, A.H., et al. 1977. The paperwork forest: Can state and local governments find a way out? *Pub. Adm. R.* 37(6):725-729.

Marino, M.F., III. 1977. The Occupational Safety and Health Act and the federal workplace: Implementation of OSHA by the Departments of Defense and the Navy. *Labor Law J.* 28(11):707-721.

Mason, J.B., and Mayer, M.L. 1975. Food industry sanitary practices: Guidelines in regulation. *MSU Bus. Topics* (Summer):47-52.

McKean, R. 1970. Products liability: Trends and implications. *U. Chicago Law R.* 38(Fall):3-63.

Momboisse, R.M. 1977. How to survive in the regulatory jungle. *Mgt. R.* (September):43-47.

Morner, A.L. 1977. Junk aid for small business. *Fortune* (November):204-214.

*Narver, J.C., contr. ed. 1976. The viability of small business in the U.S. economy. *J. Cont. Bus.* (Spring):entire issue.

Nicholas, J.R., Jr. 1973. OSHA: Big government and small business. *MSU Bus. Topics* 21(Winter):57-64.

Notes. 1977. Warrantless nonconsentual searches under the occupational safety and health act of 1970. *Geo. Wash. Law R.* 46(1):93-112.

Oi, W.Y. 1973. The economics of product safety. *Bell J. Econ.* (Spring):3-28.

Peltzman, S. 1973. An evaluation of consumer protection legislation. *J. Polit. Econ.* (September-October):1049-1091.

Posner, R.A. 1975. The social costs of monopoly and regulation. *J. Polit. Econ.* 83(4):807-827.

Reinhardt, C.F. 1977. Upgrading testing and evaluation of regulatory standards. *Res. Mgt.* 20(2):27-29.

Schmults, E.C. 1977. Evaluation of overall benefits and shortcomings of federal regulation. *Bus. Lawyer* 32(Spring):869-874.

*Schultze, C.L. 1977. The public use of private interest, *Harpers* (May):43-50, 55-62.

Silber, W.L., and Polakoff, M.E. 1970. The differential effects of tight money: An econometric study. *J. Finance* 25(March):83-97.

Solomon, H., ed. 1977. The growing influence of federal regulations. *Educ. Record* 58(Summer):270-284.

*Spriestersbach, D.C., and Farrell, W.J. 1977. Impact of federal regulations at a university. *Science* 198(4312):27-30.

Steele, J.L. 1974. O.R. models as tools for regulation of industry. *Omega-Int. J.* 2(3):335-347.

Stoll and Curley. 1970. Small business and the new issues market for equities. *J. Fin. Qu. An.* (September):309-322.

Stone, A. 1975. Business regulation-system is a problem. *Policy St. J.* 4(1):58-62.

Stuhaug, D. 1977. Don't just stand there—Undo something! *Seattle Bus.* (October 10):49-52.

Teller, B. 1977. Legislature studies Washington's liquor monopoly system. *Wash. St. Res. Council R.* (November 15).

Thayer, H.E. 1977. Business in an era of legislation and regulation. *Chem. Ind. L.* N.6:225-227.

Thieblot, A.J. 1976. How government chokes small business. *Nation's Bus.* (May):70-72.

Tinic, S.M., and West, R.R. 1976. Economics of market making—regulation versus competition. *J. Cont. Bus.* 5(3):5-70.

Walters, K.D. 1976. Beverage container regulation: Economic implications and suggestions for model legislation. *Ecology L.Q.* 5(265):265-289.

Weaver, P.H. 1977. Unlocking the gilded cage of regulation. *Fortune* (February): 179-188.

Weaver, P.H. 1978. Regulation, social policy, and class conflict. *Pub. Interest* 50(Winter):45-63.

Weidenbaum, M.L. 1975. The high cost of government regulation. *Bus. Horiz.* 18(4):43-51.

Weidenbaum, M.L. 1976. How business works for the government. *Nat. J.* (May 15):680.

Weidenbaum, M.L. 1975. Government controls over private sector: Waste, bias, stupidity, uncontrolled power. *Money Manager* 4(2).

Whitehead, J.C. 1974. SEC must drop role of industry adversary. *Money Manager* (July 1):21-22.

Wilson, J.Q. 1971. The dead hand of regulation. *Pub. Interest* 25(Fall):39-58.

1975. The "Regulators"—They cost you $130 billion a year. *U.S. News and World R.* (June 30):24-28.

1975. Are government programs worth the price? *Bus. Week* (June 30):114,116.

1975. Small business: The maddening struggle to survive. *Bus Week* (June 30):96-104.

1976. Cost of regulations: "Billions of dollars a year," interview with M.L. Weidenbaum, etc. *U.S. News and World R.* (June 14):31-34.

1977. Government intervention (special issue). *Bus. Week* (April 4):42-95.

1977. Present and future problems in governmental regulatory proliferation—A program by the committee on the year 2000. *Bus. Lawyer*, 33(1):433-474.

1978. Legal reforms for small businesses—A symposium by the small business committee. *Bus. Lawyer* 33(2):847-928.

U.S. Government Reports

*U.S. Office of the Comptroller General. *Government Regulatory Activity: Justifications, Processes, Impacts and Alternatives*. Washington D.C., June 3, 1977.

U.S. Congress, House, Joint Committee on Printing. *A History and Accomplishments of the Permanent Select Committee on Small Business*. Report to the 93d Cong., 2d sess., by Iustinus Gould, 1973.

*U.S. Commission on Federal Paperwork. *Final Summary Report*. Washington, D.C., October 3, 1977.

U.S. Commission on Federal Paperwork. *Reports and Recommendations*. 1977. Program study reports on: Energy; Environmental Impact Statements; Equal Employment Opportunity; Occupational Safety and Health; Pension Reform (ERISA); Small Business Loans; and Statistics. Government-wide reports on: Federal/State/Local Cooperation; History of What the Federal Government Has Tried to Do about Paperwork; Information Value/Burden Assessment Ombudsmen: Responding to Citizens' Problems; Records/Paperwork Management; The Role of Congress; Rulemaking; and Service Management. Impact Studies on: Federal Paperwork and State and Local Government.

U.S. Department of Commerce. *Summary of United States Department of Commerce Hearings on Regulatory Reform*. Portland, Oregon, December 11, 1975.

U.S. Department of Commerce, Bureau of the Census. *Pollution Abatement Costs and Expenditures, 1976*. Washington, D.C., Government Printing Office, 1977.

U.S. Department of Commerce, Bureau of Economic Analysis. *Survey of Current Business.*

U.S. Congress, House, Committee on Small Business, Subcommittee on Antitrust, Consumers, and Employment. *Future of Small Business in America*. Washington, D.C., Government Printing Office, 1978.

U.S. Congress, House, Committee on Small Business, Subcommittee on Capital, Investment, and Business Opportunities. *Hearings on Revitalization of Business Districts, 18 October 1977*. Washington, D.C., Government Printing Office, 1977.

U.S. Congress, House, Committee on Small Business, Subcommittee on Capital, Investment, and Business Opportunities. *Hearings on Small Business*

Access to Equity and Venture Capital. Washington, D.C., Government Printing Office, 1977.

U.S. Congress, House, Committee on Small Business, Subcommittee on Activities of Regulatory Agencies. *Regulatory Problems of the Independent Owner-Operators in the Nation's Trucking Industry (Part 1).* 1976.

U.S. Congress, Joint Economic Committee, Subcommittee on Economic Growth and Stabilization. *Foundations for a National Policy to Preserve Private Enterprise in the 1980s: A Study.* 95th Cong., 2d sess., Washington, D.C., Government Printing Office, 1977.

U.S. Congress, Senate, Committee on Governmental Affairs. *Study on Federal Regulation* V1–Regulatory Appointments, V2–Congressional Oversight, V3–Public Participation, V4–Regulatory Delay, V5–Regulatory Organization, V6–Framework for Regulation. 1977.

U.S. Congress, Senate, Committee on the Judiciary, Subcommittee on Administrative Practice and Procedure. *Hearings on the Regulatory Flexibility Act-5.* 95th Cong., 1st sess., October 7, 1977, Washington, D.C., Government Printing Office.

U.S. Congress, Senate, Select Committee on Small Business. *Report on the Federal Paperwork Burden.* 93rd Cong., 2d sess., May 28, 1974, Washington, D.C., Government Printing Office.

U.S. Congress, Senate, Select Committee on Small Business. *Hearings on Federal Reporting and Recordkeeping as It Affects Small Business.* 94th Cong., 1st sess., October 16, 1975, Washington, D.C., Government Printing Office.

U.S. Congress, Senate, Select Committee on Small Business. *Hearings on Economic Problems of Small Business in the Northwest United States.* 94th Cong., 1st sess., August 26, 1975, Washington, D.C., Government Printing Office.

U.S. Congress, Senate, Select Committee on Small Business. *Hearings on Economic Problems of Small Business in the Northwest United States.* 94th Cong., 1st sess., August 26, 1975, Washington, D.C., Government Printing Office.

U.S. Congress, Senate, Select Committee on Small Business. *Hearings on the Overregulation of Small Business before the Subcommittee on Government Regulation.* 94th Cong., 2d sess., April 26, 1976, Washington, D.C., Government Printing Office.

*U.S. Congress, Senate, Select Committee on Small Business. *Small Business and the Quality of American Life.* A compilation of source material on the relationship between small business and the quality of life, 1946-1976. 95th Cong., 1st sess., November 7, 1977, Washington, D.C. Government Printing Office.

U.S. Congress, Senate, Select Committee on Small Business. *Report on Small Business Administration 8(A) Contract Procurement Program.* 95th Cong., 1st sess., February 16, 1977, Washington, D.C., Government Printing Office.

U.S. Congress, Senate, Select Committee on Small Business. *Hearings on the Effect of Government Regulation upon Homebuilding and Related Construction*. 95th Cong., 1st sess., June 1, 1977, Washington, D.C., Government Printing Office.

U.S. Congress, Senate, Select Committee on Small Business. *Hearings on Small Business Administration Paperwork*. 95th Cong., 1st sess., September 21, 1977, Washington, D.C., Government Printing Office.

U.S. Congress, Senate, Select Committee on Small Business. *Hearings on Economic and Small Business Conditions in the Fishing Industry*, 95th Cong., 1st sess., December 5, 1977, Washington, D.C., Government Printing Office.

U.S. Congress, Senate, Select Committee on Small Business. *Twenty-Seventh Annual Report*. 94th Cong., 2d sess., February 25, 1977, Washington, D.C., Government Printing Office.

U.S. Congress, Senate, Select Committee on Small Business. *Twenty-Eighth Annual Report*. 95th Cong., 1st sess, February 1, 1978, Washington, D.C., Government Printing Office.

U.S. Department of Commerce. *Hearings on Summary of U.S. Department of Commerce Hearings on Regulatory Reform*. Portland, Oregon, December 11, 1975.

*U.S. Department of Labor, Occupational Safety and Health Administration. *Occupational Safety and Health Administration's Impact on Small Business*. Report prepared for the Assistant Secretary of Labor by OSHA's Policy Analysis and Integration Staff, July 1976.

U.S. Small Business Administration. *1974 Annual Report*. Washington, D.C., Government Printing Office, 1975.

U.S. Small Business Administration, Office of Advocacy. *The Study of Small Business (Part I)*. 1977.

*U.S. Small Business Administration, Office of Advocacy. *The Study of Small Business (Part II—What is a Small Business?)*. 1977.

U.S. Small Business Administration, Office of Advocacy. *The Study of Small Business (Part III—The Impact of Taxation on Small Business: A Proposal for Reform)*. 1977.

U.S. Small Business Administration, Office of Planning, Research, and Data Management. *Small Enterprise in the Economy*. Washington, D.C., 1977.

U.S. Small Business Administration, Office of Planning, Research, and Data Management. *Region X—Seattle/Economic Profile*. Washington, D.C., 1977.

U.S. Small Business Administration, Office of Advocacy. *The Report of the St. Louis Task Force on the Taxation of Small Business*. 1977.

Contract Research Reports, State Reports, Books, and Other Published Materials

Aaron, Carol A. 1977. *Business Migration Study: An Analysis of Out-Migration Patterns of Seattle Firms*. Institute for Puget Sound Needs for City of Seattle Department of Community Development.

Alstyne, C. van, and Coldren, S.L. 1976. *The Costs of Implementing Federally Mandated Social Programs of Colleges and Universities.* American Council on Education, Washington, D.C.

*Battelle Human Affairs Research Centers. 1978. *The Structure and Drafting of Safeguards Regulatory Documents.* Draft report, September. U.S. Nuclear Regulatory Commission, Washington, D.C.

Battelle Memorial Institute. 1978. *An Analysis of the Incentives Used to Stimulate Energy Production.* PNL-2410, September. U.S. Department of Energy, Washington, D.C.

Boeing Computer Services, Inc. 1976. *State of Washington Department of Commerce and Economic Development Evaluation of a Master Application Program for Business Licensing.* December 15.

Bosselman, Fred, et al. 1976. *The Permit Explosion—Coordination of the Proliferation.* The Urban Land Institute, Washington, D.C.

Braden, John. 1975. *The Forest Products Complex in the Economy of the Central Puget Sound Region—Analysis of Past Trends and Future Prospects.* Central Puget Sound Economic Development District, August.

*Carson, Deane, ed. 1973. *The Vital Majority: Small Business in the American Economy* (essays marking the twentieth anniversary of the U.S. Small Business Administration). U.S. Small Business Administration, Washington, D.C.

Casenave, Marx, II. 1976. "The Cost of State Paperwork Requirements to a Small Business." Assembly Office of Research, Sacramento, California.

*Charleswater Associates, Inc. 1975. *The Impact on Small Business Concerns of Government Regulations That Force Technological Change.* Final report, September. U.S. Small Business Administration, Washington, D.C.

*Chilton, Kenneth W. 1978. *The Impact of Federal Regulation on Small Business.* Center for the Study of American Business, Washington University, St. Louis, Missouri.

Clark, Douglas L. 1976. *Start a Successful Business in Washington.* Seattle: Self-Counsel Press of Oregon, Inc.

Clark, Douglas L. 1977. *Starting a Business in Washington State,* 6th ed. State of Washington Department of Commerce and Economic Development.

*Defina, Robert. 1977. "Public and Private Expenditures for Federal Regulation of Business." Working paper no. 22, Center for the Study of American Business, Washington University, St. Louis, Missouri.

Hollander, Edward D., et al. 1967. *The Future of Small Business.* New York: Praeger.

Jackson, Arlyne A. 1977. *Small Business Development and Management* (a bibliography). Harvard Business School, Cambridge, Mass.

Kahn, A.E. 1970. *The Economics of Regulation.* New York: Wiley.

Leone, Robert A., et al. 1975. *Report to the National Commission on Water Quality.* National Bureau of Economic Research. Cambridge, Mass.

Leone, Robert A. 1976. *Environmental Controls: The Impact on Industry.* Lexington, Mass.: D.C. Heath.

MacAvoy, Paul W., and Snow, Joan W., eds. 1977. *Regulation of Entry and pricing in Truck Transportation.* American Enterprise Institute for Public Policy Research, Washington, D.C.

MacAvoy, Paul W., ed. 1977. *OSHA Safety Regulation: Report of the Presidential Task Force.* American Enterprise Institute for Public Policy Research, Washington, D.C.

*McKean, Roland N. 1976. "Avoidance and Enforcement Costs in Government Regulation." Working paper no. 16, Center for the Study of American Business, Washington University, St. Louis, Missouri.

Minnesota Department of Economic Development. 1976. *Report of the Advisory Task Force on Small Business.* Final report, November 15.

National Association of Manufacturers. 1976. *Regulatory Failure–II.* A documentary of the overregulation of business by federal regulatory agencies, July.

Oregon Department of Economic Development. 1976. "Doing Business in Oregon." Portland, Oregon, April.

Peat, Marwick, Mitchell and Co. 1975. *Small Business Reporting Burden.* Prepared for the Executive Office of the President, Office of Management and Budget.

National Federation of Independent Business. *Quarterly Economic Reports for Small Business, 1975-1978.* San Mateo, Calif.

Seattle Chamber of Commerce, Research Department. "Starting a Business in the Seattle Area."

Schumacher, E.F. 1973. *Small Is Beautiful.* New York: Harper & Row.

Shepherd, William G., and Gies, Thomas G., eds. 1974. *Regulation in Further Perspective.* Cambridge, Mass.: Ballinger.

Steiner, George, ed. 1972. *Issues in Business and Society.* New York: Random House.

University of Iowa, Office of the Vice President for Educational Development and Research. 1976. *Impact of Federal Regulations on the University of Iowa.* A compilation of campuswide responses, May 24.

Washington State Commission for Vocational Education. 1975. *Job Opportunities Forecast for Washington State, 1976-1982.*

*Weidenbaum, Murray L. 1977. *Business, Government, and the Public.* Englewood Cliffs, N.J.: Prentice-Hall.

*Wilkerson, William R. 1977. *Proposals for Regulatory Reform in Washington.* Department of Commerce and Economic Development.

*1978. *Report of the Joint Interim Task Force on Small Business.* Submitted to members of the sixtieth legislative assembly, State of Oregon (MACCH).

Unpublished Articles, Papers, Memoranda, Testimony, and Speeches

Bafus, Bill. 1977. *Economic Impact Analysis––Background and Concepts.* Internal report, Washington State Department of Ecology, Olympia, Washington.

Brands, Paul A. 1977. "Change in the Inflation Impact Statement Program." Internal memorandum, January 26, U.S. Environmental Protection Agency, Washington, D.C.

Bundy, Emory. 1977. "Workings of the Bureaucratic Mind." Unpublished paper.

Miller, James C., III. 1977. *Regulatory Reform: Some Problems and Approaches.* Reprint of speech delivered December 2, 1976 before the American Management Association's First National Forum on Business, Government, and the Public Interest in Washington, D.C., American Enterprise Institute, Washington, D.C.

Shanaman, Fred C. 1977. "Can Business Stem the Tide of Federal Regulatory Legislation?" Speech given on August 12 to the Oregon Bankers Association, Lewis and Clark College, Portland, Oregon.

Vesper, Karl H. and Pederson, Arthur M. 1976. "Venture Capital Through Regulation A Public Offerings," University of Washington.

*U.S. Commission on Federal Paperwork, Small Business Study Group. 1977. *The Federal Paperwork Bureau: A Quantitative and Qualitative Assessment.* Internal draft, April 28, includes impact on small business.

Washington State Department of Commerce and Economic Development. 1976. "Business Coordination Act." Draft of legislative proposals and timetables, February.

Weidenbaum, Murray L. 1977. "Government Regulation and the Cost of Housing." Paper presented at the conference on the cost of housing, Federal Home Loan Bank of San Francisco, December 7.

Wood, Mike, 1976. "Cost Categorization: Bases for Classification," Battelle Human Affairs Research Centers, Seattle, Washington.

1977. *The Harvard Faculty Project in Regulatory Reform.* Kennedy School of Government, Harvard University. (Concept Paper plus Appendixes).

1978. Testimony of Bernard S. Browning on Small Business Impact Statement Act of 1977 to Subcommittee on Special Small Business Problems, House Committee on Small Business. Chamber of Commerce of the United States of America, Washington, D.C.

1978. Testimony of James M. Folsom, Deputy Director, Bureau of Economics, Federal Trade Commission, before the House Subcommittee on Antitrust, Consumers and Employment of the House Committee on Small Business. March 21.

1978. U.S. Department of Commerce, Bureau of the Census. Statement of Miss Shirley Kallek, Associate Director before the Subcommittee on Antitrust, Consumers, and Employment. Committee on Small Business, U.S. House of Representatives, March 22.

1978. Testimony of James C. Miller, III, co-director and resident scholar, Center for the Study of Government Regulation, American Enterprise Institute for Public Policy Research, before the Subcommittee on Special Small Business Problems. Committee on Small Business, U.S. House of Representatives, Washington, D.C., March 8.

1978. Statement of James D. "Mike" McKevitt, Washington Counsel, National Federation of Independent Businesses, before Subcommittee on Antitrust, Consumers, and Employment of the House Committee on Small Business, on the Future on Small Business in America. March 21.

1978. Statement of National Small Business Association before Subcommittee on Antitrust, Consumers, and Employment. House Small Business Committee holding hearings on the Future of Small Business in America. March 22.

About the Authors

Roland J. Cole is a research scientist at Battelle Memorial Institute's Human Affairs Research Centers. He was himself the manager of a small business (Boise Fun Spot, Inc.—a small amusement park in Boise, Idaho). Since coming to Battelle, he has specialized in the interaction of public and private organizations, largely through the study of government regulations. His other work includes *Structure and Drafting of Safeguards Regulatory Documents*, and *An Analysis of Federal Incentives Used to Stimulate Energy Production*. He is a former acting director of the Governor's Advisory Council on Urban Affairs in Washington State. His academic training includes the Ph.D. in public policy and a law degree, both from Harvard University.

Philip D. Tegeler is currently a student at Columbia Law School. He was on the staff of Advisory Services for Better Housing, a nonprofit housing assistance corporation in New York City. He was a research assistant at Battelle whose principal assignment was the project on small business. He received the A.B. from Harvard College.